Sis Goldie
God bless

┃┃┃┃┃┃┃┃┃┃┃┃┃┃┃┃┃┃┃┃┃┃┃
Ⅱ0658849

But God...

Dr. Jacqueline Rice

Elder Jackie Rice

Foreword By:
Bishop Alfred A. Owens, Jr., *D.Min.*

Copyright © 2015 by Dr. Jacqueline Rice
Library of Congress Catalog-In-Publication Data Available
Library of Congress Control Number: 1-1399894491
All rights reserved. This book or any portion thereof
may not be reproduced or used in any manner whatsoever
without the express written permission of the publisher
except for the use of brief quotations in a book review.

Printed in the United States of America

First Printing, 2015

All scriptures references are taken from the HOLY BIBLE,
MESSAGE BIBLE, NEW INTERNATIONAL VERSION®, NIV®
Copyright © 1973, 1978, 1984, 2011 by Biblica, Inc.™ Used by
permission. All rights reserved worldwide.

Published by:
MAC Publishing
www.macpub.org

BUT GOD...

ISBN-10: 0990963446
ISBN-13: 978-0-9909634-4-8

TABLE OF CONTENTS

ENDORSEMENT

In life, there are things we just cannot control and we must totally depend on God. Dr. Rice has allowed her life to be an open book to the world. We know that Satan has one assignment for our lives, and that is to steal, kill, and destroy (John 10:10). Dr. Rice articulates how the enemy targeted her life, but by God's grace, victory has won. Dr. Rice's life story is an example of what the enemy means for evil, God meant it for good (Genesis 50:20). I rejoice with Dr. Rice for the precious sacrifice of Jesus Christ on the cross. This opened the door to give the world a second chance to overcome adversity. As you read this story, be encouraged, you too can be an overcomer.

Dr. Aaron R. Jones, Senior Pastor
New Hope Church of God

FOREWORD

It is not very often that you find a vessel, as willing as Jackie Rice, who will share from the depths of her life's experience, so that others may be strengthened. In her first book release, But God: Released From a Dysfunctional Past, Jackie shares her painful, yet, victorious truth about her life's journey. She intricately reveals how her life's path began as a hopeless case that turned into a case of hope.

From the moment that Jackie's father denied her, one would say the odds seemed stacked against her. Her story, however, is a story of perseverance, compassion, redemption and victory. There is some level of dysfunction in everyone's life. Everyone makes wrong choices during the course of life. What happened to her and the choices she made could have destroyed her and those around her. It is the perseverance in her heart and the grace over her life that sustained her long enough to make better choices through God.

Jackie's approach to the revelation of her life is very intriguing, yet simple and refreshing enough to leave you wanting to know more about how her story ends. Her story, however, has not ended.

Jackie uses her story to help other women realize their own dreams and end the harsh, bitter cycle of a dysfunctional past. As the lay counselor in our church, Greater Mt. Calvary Holy Church, Washington, DC, she implements her professional training, God-shaped wisdom and life's experiences to help those who would otherwise, die daily from their own cycles of mental poverty and environmental oppression. As a licensed minister, she positions herself as an example of hope for other women who have lives in the same pattern. She gives God all glory for where she is now and Jesus has remained her anchor of hope.

I am most proud of my spiritual daughter. The courage to articulate her story will bless many lives and show others that they are not alone in the trenches of a dysfunctional past.

Because of Calvary

Bishop Alfred A. Owens, Jr., *D. Min.*
Greater Mt. Calvary Holy Church, *Senior Pastor*
Washington, DC

DEDICATIONS

This book is dedicated to the women whom God used as the catalyst for the release of my story. I shared a part of my life with you so that you would realize that you can be free from the nightmares of your past. It is my prayer that you will continue walking in your freedom.

But you were washed
But you were sanctified
But you were justified
In the name of the Lord Jesus
And by the Spirit of God

1 Corinthians 6:11 (NKJV)

This book is also dedicated to the women (and men) who will read my story and come to the realization that there is no stronghold, in your life, that cannot be broken.

Take My yoke upon you and learn from Me,
for I am gentle and lowly in heart,
and you will find rest for your souls

Matthew 11:29 (NKJV)

ACKNOWLEDGEMENTS

To Archbishop Alfred A. Owens, Jr. and Co-Pastor, Dr. Susie C. Owens, I thank God for you. Your friendship, prior to my becoming a member of the Greater Mt. Calvary Holy Church family, was the beginning of a great turning point in my life. You shared unselfishly of yourselves as you poured into my life, both spiritually and on a personal level. I cannot express my gratitude for what you have given me over the years. Thank you for allowing God to use you to sow into my life. Bishop Owens, I especially thank you for encouraging me and helping me with this project.

To Dr. Aaron Jones, you were the first to encourage me to write my story. Thank you for agreeing to endorse the book. Thank you, also, for the privilege to serve as an adjunct professor at National Bible College and Seminary.

To Elder Louise Battle, thank you for all of the professional advice and assistance that you provided as first editor. I am so grateful for your prayers and encouragement. Your enthusiasm kept me motivated. Your hard work is much appreciated.

To James, my husband and my honey, thank you for loving me unconditionally and for teaching me what real love really is. Thank you for letting me know that you will always love me. Despite my issues with life, you have always been there for me. I will always love you.

To my children, Robert, Henry, Alesia, and William, I love you so very much. When I thought that life was too much for me to handle, you were my reason for living. Although we have had to weather some storms together, our God has kept us through the power of His love for us. You are the most precious gifts that I have ever received. I thank God for giving you to me. Love you always - MOM

To ALL of my wonderful spiritual children who call me "mom" or "mother Rice", thank you for showering me with such love and respect. Each of you, in your own way, are such a blessing to me and have a very special place in my heart. Much love to you – Mom

To my church family and friends, especially to Bishop T. Cedric and Lady Bobette Brown and the Missionary Ministry, I cannot begin to express my appreciation to you for your respect, love, and prayers. I so often thank God for placing me at Greater Mt. Calvary Holy Church. I love you all.

To Mac Publishers, thank you for seeing my story as a project that your company has deemed worthy to publish. Lady McNair, thank you for your encouragement from the very beginning of our working together to complete the book.

Introduction

A s a pastoral counselor, I see many hurting women who can't seem to break free from the pain and suffering of their past. They are still feeling the effects of abuse and neglect. Week after week, as I minister to these women, I've come to believe that God has positioned me to help them release the shame and to help them find freedom from the pains of family dysfunctions that have hampered their walk with Him. The pain and suffering (mental anguish) have prevented them from fulfilling the purpose which God has ordained for their lives. Some of them believe that they are suffering, not only because of what was done to them, but also because of what they have done to themselves. While their beliefs may have some element of truth, the real truth is that they do not have to remain stuck in the quagmire of their past situations or circumstances. Although it may not be obviously apparent, they come from dysfunctional families, some of which look "picture perfect" to those who are not made privy to what goes on behind closed doors. Many of their stories sound like my story.

Thus, the reason for writing this book - I want to encourage women (and maybe some men also) to realize that no matter what they may have endured at the hands of other people or no matter what detrimental things they may have done to themselves, there is nothing that our heavenly Father cannot mend. He can fix it! He made restoration possible through His Son, Christ Jesus. Jesus came to heal the brokenhearted, to open the prison to those who are bound, to give them beauty for ashes, joy for mourning, and the garment of praise for the spirit of heaviness, that they may be called trees of righteousness (see Isaiah 61:1-3)

The story of my life is filled with so much dysfunction that I can easily relate to much of what I hear in the counseling office. **BUT GOD!!** I can personally testify that God is a healer from the effects of past abuse, mistreatment, violence or any other traumas/dramas of life (whether inflicted by others against you or self-inflicted). In this book, there is the good, the bad and the ugly of family dysfunction. Dysfunctional families breed dysfunctional children who become dysfunctional adults. **BUT GOD!!** We can be free **AND** functional through Christ Jesus. If anyone is in Christ, he [she] is a new creation: old things have passed away; behold, all things have become new (2 Corinthians 5:17).

God bless you as you read the story of my life. May you find strength and courage to know that you can be free from any ills of your past and that you can enjoy a healthy and prosperous life. As I often say to others, "God does not love me anymore than He loves you. If He did it for me (and He did!), He can do it for you."

Behold, I was shapen in iniquity; and in sin did my mother conceive me.
~Psalm 51:5~

Chapter One:
Smeared Image

Surely, I was sinful at birth, sinful from the time my mother conceived me (Psalm 51:5). How can that really be true? The Bible says that man (male and female) was created in His own image (Genesis 1:27). Since the Bible, contrary to popular belief, does not contradict itself, there has to be something that occurred between the Genesis account and the lament of David in Psalm 51.

As for me, personally, I have the same profession as David, i.e., I was sinful from birth – my mother conceived me in sin. How can I or David be correct, in light of what Geneses 1:27 says? It says that I was created in the image of God, which I should be like God, having His characteristics, receiving my identity from Him (intellect and personality, being able to see, speak, hear, relate and reason). Because of the Great "I AM", I am.

There are additional qualities and traits that reveal the image of God. He is compassionate, understanding, slow to anger, gracious, longsuffering, forgiving and truthful. He is perfect in all His Ways. He is love, full of kindness, goodness and mercy. There are so many wonderful things about Him that it would take a book to even begin to describe Him.

Now, if I am supposed to have His characteristics and if I am made in His image, something is amiss. If the Bible is right (and I truly believe that it is), how then, am I so sinful?

The answer is quite simple – my image has been smeared. I was shaped in iniquity and born in sin – born into a dysfunctional family. Let me give you a brief description of the immediate members of my biological family.

My first memories revolve around my grandmother. I lived with her and my two older sisters. My sisters were seven and five years older than me. I didn't "meet" my mother until she came to visit us. I may have been about four or five years old. My brother is 5 years younger than me. I was eight years old before I even realized that I had a brother.

I mentioned my grandmother, mother, two sisters and a brother. What about my father? That question haunted me throughout most of my adolescent and young adult life. I "met" him when I was approximately five years of age. I remember, very clearly, the brief introduction. My mother said to my father, "Meet your daughter." His response was, "She's not my daughter. She must belong to one of your other N------." I don't know why but, instantly, I felt hurt that my father didn't want me. That was my first recollection of rejection and the pain of rejection attached itself to me for many years.

I was born with a smeared image. I was one of four children, birthed by my mother who had never been married and each child had a different father. WOW!! I was born with a smeared image, passed from my mother, from her mother and the smear can be traced all the way back to the "Garden." I can't trace the root back that far. I can only go back as far as my grandmother who, by the way, conceived my mother (the youngest of her six children) outside of her marriage. I never knew my grandmother's first husband, so I don't know if he was living or dead when my mother was born. I only know, based on stories that I heard as I got older, that my mother was the "black sheep" of the family and much hated by her paternal siblings. Even some of her maternal siblings "looked down on her" as though she was beneath them. However, in the end, she was the one that they would seek out whenever they were experiencing difficulties. They were never in need of money (all of her siblings were doing well financially), but they needed something that their money could not buy –moral support and spiritual guidance. God had done a marvelous work in my mother's life and the "black sheep" became highly respected among the family members. But that's another story and I will share bits and pieces later in my story.

Before I continue with my story, I would like to talk about the dysfunctional family. I realize that I am not the only one born into a dysfunctional family. All of us have been. Take a good look at the families around us. When we see the individual family unit, none of us can deny that there is some dysfunction within each of our families. I dare say that none of us are perfect. We were all born in sin and shaped in iniquity. Hence, the result is the existence of dysfunctional families.

Dysfunction - what does it mean? It is defined as something which is abnormal or impaired; something is wrong – it doesn't operate as it was intended to operate – it's out of order. The word dysfunction is used synonymously with the word malfunction, i.e., to function improperly or failure to function. Therefore, again, I say look at the families that you know – starting with your own immediate family. The normal family unit, as God intended it, consists of two parents (father and mother), children, grandchildren, aunts, uncles, nieces, nephews, cousins, etc. This family, if it were functioning normally, would be loving and kind to one another, looking out for the welfare of each other, worshipping God together, and living in peace and harmony with each other. That's a far cry from what we see today. Too often, the family unit is just the opposite. Family members hating and killing each other; drugs, alcohol, and sexual addictions; incest; abandonment; abuse; all types of evidence that indicates that something, or rather someone, is not functioning properly. Something is wrong! Where is the love? Where is the peace? Where is compassion? I submit to you that it has been smothered by a drastic disease called sin.

We should not be surprised that there are so many dysfunctional families among us. After all, God – the Father of us all, has the most dysfunctional family ever. What we are witnessing today is just a trickle-down effect. We are all members of one family. God is our Father. From the very beginning, God instituted family. The family structure is the masterpiece of God's creative work. When He created the heavens, the earth, the sun, moon, and stars, when He made the animals, fish and fowl, the trees and plants, the rivers and seas, He looked at them and said that it was good. Then He made Man in His own likeness and image, looked at him and said that he was VERY GOOD! He gave Man a wife and told them to be fruitful and multiply. Adam and Eve, the first man and woman, the first couple united in holy matrimony, became the first parents of the first family. Behold God's masterpiece.

It was God's intention that this family, which was made in His image, would continue to increase so that the world would be filled with people who would inherit the earth (in its original stage). He wanted them to be like Him, having all of His attributes. He wanted them to be loving and kind, compassionate, caring and merciful. He wanted them to look like Him and act like Him. After all, they were His children.

However, the very first family became a dysfunctional family. They did not function as God created them to function. His image in them was smeared. Check it out. In chapter three of the book of Genesis (the book of beginnings) the first couple who became the first parents, committed the first sin – disobedience. The first son of the first parents murdered his first sibling and became the first to be banned from the family unit and, as a result, became the first homeless person. By the time we reach chapter six, the descendants of the first family had become so wicked that God said, "I've had enough. I will destroy them" (my translation). But God was so into having a family that He looked among the people and saw Noah. The Bible describes Noah as being a just man, who was perfect in his generation.

Thus, Noah was chosen to be the one who would provide God with a new family. Once again, we hear God saying, "Be fruitful and multiply." And, once again, history repeated itself. Noah goes into a drunken stupor and when he awakens, the first thing he does is put division among the family unit by placing a curse upon his younger son, Canaan. Once again, the behavior of men took a downward spin. They became continually evil in their ways, not knowing how to or were unwilling to walk according to God's standards.

But God still wanted a family. He decided to choose or call out of the established nations, one family unit – Abraham and his family. Thus, the Jewish nation was established as the nation that God sat apart for himself. Nonetheless, despite their efforts to serve God, they continued to be a dysfunctional family. They would serve Him for a while and then return to their old ways. They would get in trouble and run back to Him and the cycle kept repeating itself.

Despite the behavior of his children, God remained determined to have a family who would portray His image. He wrapped a part of Himself up and placed it in the womb of a virgin girl who gave birth to His only perfect son (since Adam). This son walked among the people to show them how to be the sons and daughters that they were created to be. God loved these people so much that He allowed His Son, Jesus, to become a ransom for their sins so that they may have life eternally.

From generation to generation, even down to today's generation, sin runs rampant throughout the world. Nonetheless, God's love keeps reaching out to us, pleading with us to acknowledge Him as our Father. However, it saddens me to say that I believe that sin is greater now than it has ever been. There are dysfunctional families everywhere. The sin within each dysfunctional family unit filters out all over the world.

BUT GOD!! The end is not yet. What He created, He can fix. It's not over until God says that it's over and He will have His family as He desires. When the wickedness of this world is dispelled and the Son of God comes again, He will gather many of us and carry us to that place that He has prepared for us. There, we will spend eternity with our Father and enjoy the pleasures of a perfectly functional family. I'll tell you more about that later.

Train a child in the way he should go, and when he is old he will not turn from it.
~Proverbs 22:6~

CHAPTER TWO:
Early Childhood Development

I was born in Washington, DC. However, I lived with my grandmother (Mama) and two sisters in a rural town in North Carolina. The early memories of my childhood probably go back to when I was four or five years old. The house in which we lived was the typical "box" house - what I like to refer to as the 4X4 - four rooms (three bedrooms and the kitchen) all of equal size. I can still visualize that house and have some very fond memories of it. The two front bedrooms and the kitchen were the only rooms that we used for our routine activities. The third bedroom (on the back side of the house) was next to the kitchen. In that room was an old dresser and a cast iron bed with a straw mattress. I often used it as my "play room." On Saturday evenings, it was used as a "bathroom." We would go through our weekly ritual of bringing water into the house and heating it on the cast iron stove in the kitchen so that we could take our baths. Yes, that's right – only one bath a week. Can you imagine? But, I guarantee you that none of us were dirty or smelly the rest of the week. That was absolutely not allowed! During the remainder of the week, we would get up and put water in a "face basin" and wash our bodies. We used baking soda and salt to brush our teeth. At bedtime, we would repeat the morning hygiene.

By now, I'm sure that you have determined that we were very poor. That's true, but my sisters and I didn't know it. Let me try to describe how poor we were, based on today's standard of living. I think that we had less than most of the other families in our community. We didn't have a "living room" because there was no electricity in the third bedroom that I called my playroom. We would go in that room at night (using a flash light) only if it was absolutely necessary. I remember going into the room one night and seeing my reflection in the window. I ran out screaming to my grandmother that someone was outside looking into our house. I had no clue that that someone outside looking in was me. There was no running water in the house. However, we were blessed to have a spigot in the back yard instead of having to go to a well for drinking water or to the creek for washing water, as did some of our neighbors.

There was a cast iron stove in the kitchen and a pot belly stove in the two front bedrooms. In the summer wood was used in the kitchen. If it was extremely hot, mama would cook on a two burner kerosene stove. Wood and coal was used in the stoves in the winter. We would always know when cold weather was near. My grandmother would order wood and coal and when it was delivered, it would be dumped at the top of the steps that led to the pathway in the back of our house. My sisters and I would have to get buckets and pick up the coal and carry it, along with the wood, to the front of the house where it was stored next to the cellar under our house. We would not put it in the cellar because mama was afraid that going into the dark cellar would result in a snake bite. When it actually began to get cold, mama would buy a bag of oranges. That was good and bad news. I hated oranges because there was always a dose of castor oil (to keep us from catching colds) that came with them.

Although there was some electricity in the house, the only appliances that we had was a refrigerator and a wringer type washing machine. Mama also had a radio with a record player that had to be wound up before she could play the one record that she owned. The furniture was decent but not fancy. We had to heat our iron on the wood stove. The "ironing board" was a plank that was supported on the back of a chair at each end of it. There was no inside plumbing.

Therefore, we had outhouses. That in itself was an experience. We had to always look for snakes and spiders before using them. Mama made sure that the outhouse was kept as clean as possible. I saw a few spiders on occasions but I never saw a snake around or near the outhouse.

Pre-School

There was no such thing as pre-school as far as the educational system was concerned. You had to be a certain age before you were allowed to step into the classroom as a student. Therefore, pre-school consisted of what you learned from your family and surroundings before you were old enough to attend school.

So what was my early childhood education like? I learned the basics of how to wash and dress myself, tie my shoes, feed myself, say prayer and grace, etc. I learned how to make up beds and sweep floors, clean the yard, help wash clothes, mostly by watching my sisters and grandmother. Some things I learned early because my sisters were always tricking me into thinking that their work was a lot of fun. I learned how to iron before I was six years old. My sisters would stand me up on a box and "let me" iron but I couldn't tell my grandmother. Of course, they would never let my grandmother see me iron because that was dangerous for a child my age. They told me that if mama found out that I was ironing, we would get in trouble. On wash days, my sisters would "let me" help fill up the big tin tubs with water that was used to rinse the clothes. I was so impressed with my "ability to learn" that I would go to school and just sit in the classroom. I went to school so much that the teacher finally allowed me to participate with the other children. There was only one problem with that – I was always late getting there and when I arrived, the teacher would have the other children sing the song called "Lazy Bones."

I also learned some negative things during my pre-school education. I learned that grown people liked to keep secrets from little children. But, I wanted to know what they were saying when they wanted me to "go somewhere and play." So, I learned how listen when they thought that I wasn't.

I learned how to tell lies and steal (or maybe that came naturally as a part of my smeared image). I remember an occasion when I asked my grandmother for money to buy candy and she told me that she didn't have any money. A few days later, I found some money in the dresser drawer that was in my "playroom." Don't ask me how I learned to reason that if Mama didn't have money, then, I wouldn't be taking it from her. So, I took a dollar from the handkerchief that the money was in. There was a problem, however, with my reasoning. I knew that I was wrong for taking the money and I lied when my aunt asked me where I got money to buy candy. She knew that I was "telling a story" (lying) and kept asking me about it and I kept telling her that I found it.

Now, to understand the dilemma that I was in, you would have to understand that back in those days, a dollar went a long way. I had bought more than I could eat and still had seventy-five cents left. I couldn't think of another way to get rid of the money so I threw it away. Why? One thing that I learned very early was that even though most folks did not have a telephone, news travelled quickly. Sure enough, by the time I got home, my grandmother had gotten the news that I was spending money. But the seventy-five cents had "found its way" into an unkempt plot of land in front of our house that was overgrown with weeds and bushes. Mama had already discovered that I took the money from the drawer and threatened to beat me if I didn't tell her what I did with it. So I had to confess. Then, there was another problem. When she sent me to look for the money that I threw away, I could only find the quarter.

I don't remember if Mama beat me. What I do remember is that I learned a lesson that I will never forget: When you do bad things, it does not only hurt you, it hurts those that you love. A few nights later, I woke up hearing my grandmother crying. My uncle had arrived late that night from DC. I put on the listening skills that I had learned and heard her tell him that I took some of the money that she had to pay for the house and the man would not take a partial payment. Imagine that! One dollar was about to get us evicted and worse yet, it was my fault. I was too young to understand that we were about to be put out of "our" house but, I did understand that I made my mama cry. I felt bad every time I thought about it. That feeling was worse than any beating that she could have ever given me.

There was something else that I learned as a preschooler. I didn't know it at the time, but it is called compassion. There was a lady that lived across from us and she had a baby that was born with a "water-head." I would go over to her house and help her with him because his head was so big that he could not sit up or turn over. We didn't have electric fans then. I would go to her house just to fan the flies off of him with newspaper or give him his bottle. I did not fully understand many of the things that I learned in those early years until I was much older. In some cases I was an adult before the secrets were revealed to me. In the case of this woman and her baby, it was said that during a church meeting, she became angry with the pastor and called him a "water head SOB" and as a result, the child that she was pregnant with at the time was born with the defect. I don't know how true the story is but I do know that at the age of nine, that child could not do anything for himself. I don't know when or how he learned to walk and talk, but the story continued to indicate that he was cursed from his mother's womb. He grew to become an adult, but could not speak a complete sentence without swearing.

I also learned a little about the difference between boys and girls. The little that I learned was simply this: Boys and girls could not play together unless they were in sight of the adults. You could not go to the outhouse with boys because they were not supposed to see under your dress and you were not supposed to see what was in their pants. What??? Weren't all children alike??? I learned that I should never allow a boy to put his hand under my dress. That piece of education came after I was informed that I could no longer play with my cousin. He was approximately two years older than me. He would come to our house or I would go to his house to play. We would play with horse shoes, shoot marbles, try to kill frogs, climb trees, and challenge each other with rock throwing or racing. Big fun!

Suddenly, fun with my cousin was brought to an abrupt end for reasons (as stated above) that I could not understand. I really missed playing with him. There was no one else to play with. Well, I found out why. Yep – you guessed it – my listening skills. I hear my grandmother's sister (my cousin's grandmother) telling her what had happened. Evidently his parents had not been careful enough to prevent him from observing their bedroom activities. He was a classic example of "every shut eye ain't sleep." He saw much and apparently saw often. His grandmother told my grandmother that he had been "showing manly actions", i.e., pulling up girls dresses or trying to get them to remove their "bloomers" (underwear), or he would peek into outhouses when he knew that the occupant was a girl. My grandmother was told to "keep him away from me." He was a "bad" boy.

Early childhood development also included observing the law of segregation. At such an early age, the word "segregation" was foreign to me. I had never heard the word and had no idea what it meant until several years later. However, I did learn the principle of the word. The primary thought was that "colored" people were different than the "white" people in more ways than the color of their skin.

There were certain boundaries that I was not allowed to cross if no one was with me. I could go anywhere alone, as long as I stayed in the "colored" section of town. The "coloreds" could not go to school with the "whites." If there was a back door to any of the places that my grandmother shopped, we had to use it. The "whites" were allowed to come into stores and be served before any of the "coloreds" who were already in the store. We could not sit at the counter in the drug store and eat our occasional ice cream treat. We had to take it with us. When my grandmother took me to work with her, we had to go in the back door. The lady of the house would fix lunch for us, but we had to eat at a tiny table in the corner of the kitchen while she ate alone in the dining room.

There were separate sections in the movie theater. The "colored" people had to sit upstairs in the balcony. Sometimes we would deliberately drop things down on those below us (my sisters taught me that). However, we had to make sure that it was time to leave so that we would not get put out before the movie was finished.

At the train/bus depot, the "whites" sat on one side and the "coloreds" stood on the other. Sometimes, my grandmother would have to ride the bus to the next town. She would always take me straight to the back of the bus. One day I asked why she always did that and her response was that I could see better if I looked out of the back window. That was fine with me, so, I never though anymore about it until I learned about segregation after I came to live with my mother in DC.

Entertainment

For the most part, I had to entertain myself. I would build houses with bottle caps, plait grass and make mud pies. Sometimes, I would go to the creek and try to catch tadpoles. At other times, I would visit a neighbor that I thought could make the best biscuits in the world. I would go up to her house and play in her yard, looking for four-leaf clovers or catching June bugs. My grandmother would listen to stories on the radio every day during the week. When those stories came on, I had to be quiet or go outside so that Mama could hear. Sometimes I would sit and listen with her. In the evenings, there was a kid's program called "Uncle Remus." That was the highlight of my entertainment.

Quite often, I would sit on the steps of the front porch and watch the clouds roll by. As I watched them, I would imagine that I saw them take the form of pictures. This memory always reminds me of the very vivid imagination that I've always had. Let me try to explain: I did not have books like our little children now have. The only pictures that I can remember seeing were a few pictures of people I knew or maybe pictures of cars, houses, etc. hanging on the walls of the drug store. Somehow, I had the ability to picture things that I would hear about. The stories that I heard were generally Bible stories that were taught in Sunday School. There would be days when I would look up into the clouds and "see" chariots, lambs, lions, and many other images of things that I had never seen before, including the image of Jesus. I could sit for what seemed like hours and watch those characters go by. It was not until two or three years later, when I went to live with my aunt in New York, that I realized that the images that I saw in the clouds, were the same as those that I saw in books that I then received at school.

As much as I enjoyed seeing those images, there was one that I feared. I never saw it in the day time (although I often looked for it). It would always appear in the early morning. I would awaken just as darkness was rolling away and it was cloudy. I could see outside from a space between the window and the shade. As I lay in bed, that cloud would appear, looking like a utility post. It would change in form to look like a giant size man (looking like a giant size Pillsbury Doughboy, which had not even been heard of at the time) and it would always come towards me, walking up the steps of the front porch. My heart would start pounding and I would be so afraid that I couldn't move or make a sound. That thing would come toward my window but just before it reached the window, I would be able to move from my frozen position of fear and hide my face under the bed covers. I don't know why this vision was so different than the others but I began to associate it with the "boogeyman" that I had begun to hear about. You know – "the boogeyman is going to get you if you don't be a good girl/boy." You would think that something like that would have made me do all that I could to be good, but I guess my smeared image made it easier to do wrong.

At this point, I have shared memories from my early childhood up to approximately six years old. The same year that I took the money from my grandmother, I came to DC. I don't know if this was coincidence or not. I remember that trip as my first train ride. I was excited because my sisters had come to DC about a year before that time. I was a little uneasy about traveling by myself but Mama assured me that it was okay. She packed me a good lunch and gave me some papers to give to her cousin who was to meet me at the train station in Greensboro, NC. Well that went well until after we got to his house and he left me by myself while he went to a ball game. I was so afraid that I didn't move from his kitchen table until he returned to take me back to the train station to make the connection for DC. I don't recall who met me when I got to DC but I do remember my uncle taking me out to meet some of his friends in the neighborhood. It was dark and there were funny looking little people, wearing funny looking clothes, running around the streets. When we got to my uncles' friends' house, they gave me bags of candy and money. Yes, you guessed it – it was Halloween, something that I knew nothing about and nobody explained it to me. The next day, everyone I saw looked normal. Therefore, I figured that the people that I had seen the night before, were boogeymen.

After coming to DC, my mother and I would often be at my aunt's home. I'm not sure if we lived with her or if my aunt was my "baby sitter" while my mother worked. I was often there when my mother was not. I thought that my aunt and uncle were some of the nicest people that I knew at the time. They treated me just like my grandmother treated me. Both of them usually gave me whatever I asked for. I could hardly believe that I could have an ice cream cone almost every day. My aunt would make big chocolate or checker board cakes just because I wanted some. She introduced me to foods that I'd never had before, i.e., Briggs half smokes (they had to be Briggs), toast, popsicles, pickles, and plenty of goodies. She had a television that had shows all day (not just evenings with Amos and Andy or Art Linkletter). There were shows designed just for kids. I especially liked to watch the Howdy Doody Show.

During my stay with my aunt and uncle, I learned a new lesson. Grown people not only kept secrets from children, they kept them from each other. My uncle had secrets to share with me that he didn't want me to share with anyone else. He liked to put his hand under my dress. I liked secrets, but I was confused. My grandmother had taught me never to let a boy put his hands under my dress. But this wasn't a boy. This was my uncle. I was also taught that I had to obey whatever adults said and my uncle said that I couldn't tell anybody about our secret. He would always manage to get me alone, by myself. Sometimes, with my aunt in the house, he would take me into the kitchen and put his hand under my dress. Other times, he would take me for a ride and park somewhere so that he could "play" under my clothes. I knew that it was wrong, but he said that I could not tell anyone. I didn't tell because, after all, he was an adult that I was supposed to obey.

Shortly after coming to DC, I was sent to live with another aunt in New York. I was sad to leave but also happy because I didn't like the secret that I shared with my uncle. So much for early childhood development. The memories of my first six years of life were both good and bad, but most of them were good.

Even a child is known by his deeds, whether what he does is pure and right.
~Proverb 20:11~

CHAPTER THREE:
Early Childhood Education

My official school year began at the age of six when I went to live with my aunt in New York. My first day at school was not a good one. My teacher was walking back and forth as she talked to us. When she passed my desk, she hit me in the head with the big book that she was carrying. She didn't stop talking or walking. When she passed my desk again, she asked me why I was crying. I told her because she hit me. She told me that she did not hit me and she would send me home if I didn't stop crying. I never could make myself like that teacher. I didn't say much in her class and she still was not kind. I was glad to be out of her class.

My aunt's house was very big. My cousin and I shared a room that was situated right off of the dining room. The dining room was used only for doing homework. The living room was huge with beautiful furniture and a large Baby Grand piano. The only time that we used the living room was for a very brief time on Christmas morning to open gifts. There were three floors to the house, excluding the basement. I was not allowed in those areas.

The first year with my aunt was a lot different than what I was used to. My aunt gave me a lot of things but, she was a very strict disciplinarian. We went through the same routine day after day, except for most Fridays. That was movie night.

I remember how cool it was when I went to New York. My aunt took me to get new clothes. I had never had any dresses as pretty as the ones she bought. She made it very clear that I had better not get dirty or "mess up" my new clothes. Among the items of clothing that she bought me was a red and blue sweater with real pennies for buttons. Once again, I found myself in trouble for stealing. This time I "lost" the money. I had removed one of the pennies from the sweater to buy a piece of candy. Thus, my first introduction to my aunt's method of corporal punishment – a metal spatula.

It did not take long for me to learn to go to school alone. My cousin was charged with the task of seeing that I got to and from school safely. I think that she didn't like me very much. It may have been that she resented that she had to share her room with me. She was okay with taking me to school until we got within a block away. She would then make me walk either in front of or behind her. She told me that I should not talk with any of her friends. Once again, I experienced the feeling of rejection. I could not understand why my life was changing so much.

I had to make a serious adjustment to my palate. Most of the food did not appeal to me at all! I was introduced to new food, but I was not interested in any of it. There were vegetables that I had never seen, i.e., Brussels sprouts, squash, asparagus, and spinach. The meats were mostly boiled with little seasoning. Unfortunately, I did not have the privilege to refuse any food that I did not or could not develop a taste for. The rule was to eat everything on your plate – no exceptions. I dreaded the dinner hour. I could almost always count on being sent to my room hungry. Of course, dessert was totally out of the question. Two incidences regarding my disdain for my aunt's choice of food stand out in my memory. The first was when I took a sandwich that was intended to be my lunch, and put it in the garbage can that belonged to the lady who rented the third flood in my aunt's house. She promptly told my aunt when she found the sandwich. The other incident was when I blatantly refused to eat my dinner which consisted of boiled fish and some of the vegetables that I hated (I don't remember which). Every attempt that I made to eat that fish ended up with me making a mad dash to the bathroom. As hard as I tried, I could not hold it down. For throwing away the sandwich, I was wacked with the spatula on my thighs. For not eating my dinner that night, my aunt left me sitting at the table with orders not to move until I had eaten. The rest of the family went to the movies and I sat at the table, refusing to eat, until they returned. I was given the same spatula treatment and sent to bed.

Another issue that was considered to be a disciplinary problem was the fact that I sucked my fingers. I don't know when I started the "nasty habit", but I do remember that my grandmother had tried to stop it when I lived with her. She made small cloth pockets and filled them with dirt (red clay) and tied them on my fingers, thinking that I would not want to put it in my mouth. WRONG! I resisted for a while, but at some point during the day, I had to have my finger in my mouth. (I guess that was my security blanket). Now that I think about it, I may have picked up that habit from one of my sisters. Mama didn't really want me sucking on dirt, so she didn't try that again. The next attempt to stop the finger sucking was to coat it with some type of hot paste. I gradually got used to the taste, so that method only lasted a day. However, my aunt was smarter (or more cruel) than my grandmother when it came to discipline. I would stop sucking my finger during the day but would go back to it at night/bedtime. One night, my uncle came into our bedroom and wrapped pieces of hard plastic on the inside bend of my arms. By morning, the plastic had been broken by my efforts to bend my arm in order to get my finger in its "proper place." The next night he wrapped a 2X4 piece of wood block in the bend of each arm. This cruel, painful method broke the habit overnight.

My cousin and I were not allowed to fight. Therefore, when she was annoyed with me, she would tease me, knowing that I would finally do something to get myself in trouble. As a result, since we were not allowed to fight, I would break something that belonged to her. She liked the idea, so we would have "silent fights" via breaking things that belonged to each other. That worked out fine until my aunt caught me in the act of breaking something.

What does all of this have to do with education? Those things stand out more than anything else in my first school year. As far as I can determine, I did well in school. It was the other things that I learned at home that I remember most.

I Almost Died

Sometime during the winter, I almost died. My memory of this event is only before my hospitalization and after getting well. I remember my aunt waking me during the night, but I could not stay awake. I could not get up. The next thing that I remembered was my uncle carrying me out to a black van that looked like a hearse. He put me in the van and a man (I guess a doctor?) was looking into my eyes with a light. I also remember hearing sirens and then being in a room with my uncle and a doctor. The doctor stuck my arm with something that looked like an old fashioned ink pen - the type that had to be filled with ink by drawing the ink into the pen from a bottle. (I later learned that the "ink pen" was used to draw blood from my arm.) I must have been really sick because the next thing that I remembered was being in a hospital bed. I didn't know how long I had been there. My aunt came to the hospital and told me that the hospital was a long way from home and that I would have to stay there for a while and that she would be back when I was well enough to come home.

A couple of days later, I kept asking for water and the nurse got tired of bringing it to me, so she brought me a pitcher full so that I could get it when I wanted to. I kept drinking water and lost memory of anything else until I woke up hearing the doctor screaming at the nurse. I was not aware, at the time, that I had not fallen asleep. I had passed out as a result of a high fever. My aunt came to see me the next day and told me that I would have to stay in the hospital a few more days because I had drank too much water and was sick again. Not fully understanding, to this day, I do not like to drink water. During her visit, my aunt asked me if I had eaten all of my candy. I didn't know what she was talking about. She told me that she had left candy with the nurse on her prior visit. I never saw the candy, but the nurse had given me some cookies. My aunt was furious. The reason that she became so angry about the candy was because "the nurses had taken my candy (which was very expensive) and given me some cheap cookies."

I did not learn the details of my illness until I was almost ten years old. I heard my aunt talking with my mother about it after I had come back to DC to live with my mother. I guess that it was another secret that they wanted to keep from me. I did not learn all of the details but I learned enough to know that I had almost died. Apparently, I had been diagnosed with "a touch of scarlet fever." They had no idea how I could have possibly contracted it. The day before I was to be released from the hospital, my temperature became very high (the reason for me wanting so much water). According to my aunt, the nurse should have known to check my temperature, but she never did. I ended up in another crisis for almost a week. My aunt made sure that the nurse was removed from her position. Twice, I could have died, during that illness, **BUT GOD!!!**

There was another issue with the hospital. I was placed in a room directly across the hall from a boy who was being treated for lice in his head. He would tell me almost every day that he was going to throw one of his "bugs" at me. I told my aunt and that was more fuel for my aunt's anger. I'm not sure, but I got the impression that my aunt made such a fuss about these issues, that she did not have to pay the hospital bill.

Good Times

Those days were not all bad. Some things I actually looked forward to. It snowed in New York like I had never seen before. In North Carolina, as much as I can recall, snow barely covered the ground. In New York, snow would often come half way up our legs. Both, my cousin and I loved the snow. Twice a month on Sundays, we would walk to our cousin's house. She was an adult who lived in New Jersey and the visit to her house was one of the highlights of our day. On one of those Sundays, it started snowing just before we started to go back home. It fell fast and heavy – so heavy that we could barely walk or see. That day, I began to believe that my aunt really did care about us. She was home alone with our little cousin and could not come to look for us when we didn't get home when we should have. When we finally did arrive, it was very obvious that she was really upset and afraid that something bad had happened to us. She was so happy to see us, I think that she was actually crying.

My aunt gave us candy twice a year – Christmas and Easter. We were not allowed to eat a lot of candy. By the time we finished eating Christmas candies, it was almost Easter. Easter was the highlight of the warm weather. The major spring event was the "Easter Bonnet Parade" which actually passed directly in front of our home. The ladies were decked out from head to toe (with emphases on their hats) and looked absolutely beautiful as they "strutted" to the music being played by the band.

By now, you must know that I always found a way to get on the wrong side of my aunt. I had spent almost two years with my aunt. The last Easter was probably what made her decide to send me back to my grandmother. She had bought us candy. Our baby cousin was not old enough to eat his, so my aunt set it on the dining room table. It was almost the end of the school year. My cousin and I had eaten all of our Easter candy, but my baby cousin's giant size chocolate bunny was still sitting on the dining room table. Every day, I was alone when I came home from school. You guessed it.

There I was stealing again. I was good at it too! I would carefully open the box at the bottom and break off the bottom of the bunny. That bunny was probably the last straw for my aunt. When she decided to give the candy to me and my cousin, she discovered that there was a considerable amount of the bunny missing. When the school year was over, I was on my way back to "visit" with my grandmother for the summer. I did not return to New York. When the summer vacation was over, I was sent to DC to live with my mother. Apparently, I was "too bad" for my aunt.

Foolishness is bound up in the heart of a child. The rod of correction will drive it far from him.
~Proverb 22:15~ NKJ

CHAPTER FOUR:
New Beginnings

My living arrangements seemed to have always been like a revolving door – from my grandmother in North Carolina to my aunt and uncle in DC, to my aunt in New York, back to my grandmother in North Carolina, and then back to DC with my mother and sisters. My sisters didn't seem too happy when I arrived at my aunt's house after my summer vacation with mama. Nonetheless, I was very happy to be back because I knew that my aunt would give me almost anything that I wanted. However, the happiness did not last very long. I found out that I would not be staying with my aunt. I would be living with my mother and sisters, but it turned out to be okay. We visited my aunt often, so I didn't mind staying with my mother.

My mother's house was not by any means like the other houses that I had lived in previously. It was like a rooming house. We stayed in one large room and shared a bathroom with the other people who lived in the house. There was plenty of space in that large room. It appeared as though the house was divided in half with units on each side of the stairway (like an efficiency apartment). The stove, refrigerator, and a cabinet for utensils and food storage was in one corner. The dining table sat on the same side and was positioned slightly toward the middle of the room. On the adjoining side wall was a sofa bed and other living room furniture. On the side directly across from the "kitchen" area was the bedroom furniture. In spite of all of the furniture in this one room, it really was large enough for us to be comfortable. I slept with my mother and my sisters slept on the sofa bed. On weekends, my brother would come to stay with us.

This was a new beginning for me with new learning experiences. Living with my mother and sisters was pretty much routine, as far as I could determine. There were rules and chores that really didn't seem to be too bad. Each of us had to make sure that our living quarters were kept clean at all times. Everything had its place and everything had to be in its place.

My mother was an excellent cook and I was thrilled, beyond expression, by the types of meals that she prepared. What she prepared may have been the same ordinary food that anyone else would prepare, but it tasted ooh, so good! We ate the best of whatever my mother decided to put on the table and there was always enough to spare. I would often hear my mother say, "Keep their stomachs full and they will have no excuse to steal." In addition, mother's job as a cook for a family that lived in an affluent Georgetown area gave her an extra advantage. She shopped for our food at the same places that she shopped for her employer's food. The meats and produce were guaranteed to be fresh. On Saturdays, she would shop at the farmer's market for items that were relevant to our culture, i.e., slab bacon, country sausage, large double yoke eggs, pig feet, chitterlings, etc.

We would almost always know what was for dinner on any day of the week. Usually, on Saturday, we would have hot dogs with pork and beans. Sunday morning breakfast consisted of salt herring (I didn't like those), grits or rice, and hot biscuits. Dinner would be greens or green beans, a starch (which was determined by what the meat was), and chicken or a roast. On Monday (and sometimes Tuesday) we ate what was left over from Sunday. For the remainder of the week, we had a variety of different entrees, which almost always included neck bones and beans. Of course, on Friday, we had fish.

Hilarious Disasters

On Saturday mornings, my mother would go to the market and back home, usually before my sisters and I were out of bed. She would get busy in the kitchen and we would get busy cleaning – changing bed covers, dusting furniture, mopping and waxing the floor. Our floor (a linoleum rug) would shine like new money. With a fresh application of wax on the floor, Saturday afternoons meant that you either went outside or you found a place to sit for about a half-hour until the floor dried. I mention this because I want to share an incident that made my sisters and I laugh ourselves to tears whenever we talked about it over the course of the following years, well into our adulthood. (Before I get into the incident, I would like to clarify how you can determine which sister I am talking about. My oldest sister will be just that – my oldest sister. The sister between my oldest sister and I will be my sister or my other sister.)

On one of our routine Saturdays, my sister had just finished waxing the floor and was going upstairs to wash out the mop and bucket. Mother was outside talking with the upstairs neighbor and my sister decided to eavesdrop (I guess that I wasn't the only one who liked secrets). When my mother turned to come into the house, my sister made a mad dash into our unit and tried to grab a book from me so that she could pretend that she had been sitting down as my oldest sister and I were. When she reached for the book, she missed her aim and simultaneously lost her footing on the freshly waxed floor. She fell and her arm went through my mother's glass top coffee table. She cut her arm but it was not really serious. My sister put on a performance that would have won her an Oscar. She sat in the floor going from screaming to near fainting while squeezing her arm so that more blood would come out. She wouldn't allow my mother to touch the wound without declaring that she was dying. To top off her performance, she claimed that I made her fall!

This Oscar Award winning performance was motivated by fear. My mother had a set of coffee and end tables that had a beautiful shade of royal blue glass tops. My mother warned us, on many occasions, that there would be a great price to pay if any of us broke those glass tops. She would tell us, "If you break the table, give your heart to God because you backside will belong to me." Now, you have to understand that my mother never threatened us, but she did make promises that she seldom failed to keep. She had a razor strap with splits on the end of it that put the fear of, not God, but mother, in all of us. Trust me, when I tell you – she seldom had to use it. The thought of my mother using the strap that day was what made my sister "lose it."

We knew that my mother was angry. She was not the type who yelled at us. She would get a certain look on her face (like a quick "glint" in her eye) and she would not say much. Whatever she said would be in a slow low tone. I think that we would have rather that she yelled instead. She cleaned my sister's wound while my oldest sister cleaned up the glass and blood from the floor. The first order of business, after the clean-up, was to find out who was responsible for the chaos. Fortunately, for me, it was determined that I was not! My mother was satisfied that it was just an accidental fall. WHEW!!

My sister's dilemma was not the only event that gave us tear-jerking laughter as we remembered events that really were not funny when they actually took place. Let me continue with another episode of the blue glass table that occurred prior to my sister's "down fall." My Saturday chore was to dust all of the furniture that I could reach. One Saturday, I was slow in getting the dusting completed. Mother had to go somewhere and told me that I had better be finished when she returned. Shortly after she left, a parade passed our house. I hadn't seen a parade since I lived in New York. I stopped dusting and took a seat in the windowsill to watch the parade. My sister kept teasing me – telling me that my mother was coming. After she had done this two times, I didn't believe her the third time. My mother was actually in the room when I responded, "So what, I don't care if she is coming." OOPS!! There she was!! And she didn't come alone.

She had the strap! Before I could get out of the window and back to dusting, she had me by my arm. I tried to get away from her by attempting to get to the other side of the coffee table. There was a brief period of my trying to escape by running around the table. My sister was enjoying it all. As I went around the table, she was doing a "play by play" – "airplane number one, airplane number two, uh oh – crash landing!" I fell almost into my mother's arms on my third attempt to get around the table. She promptly applied the remedy for my not caring and trying to escape.

The next event was actually a two-part that started with my oldest sister and I. She was the only one of us who had the door key. I was always the first to arrive home from school. One day, my sister was extremely late getting home and I was getting extremely restless while waiting for her. I could not leave the house. I had to sit on the steps and wait. She and my other sister finally arrived together. I was really upset and promptly "got in her face." She pushed me aside and unlocked the doors. When we got inside, I rose up again. "What took you so long?" I screamed at the top of my lungs – right in her face. She responded with a fist in my face. My nose bled so much that the upstairs neighbor called my mother to come home from work. When she arrived, they were still packing and unpacking my nose. It wouldn't stop bleeding (even with a home remedy of putting a piece of a brown paper bag under my upper lip) and my mother had to take me to the hospital. Needless to say that by the time we came back from the hospital, my mother was more than angry. I went to bed and my mother was sitting at the dressing table, rolling her hair and fussing with my oldest sister. She was sitting across the room on the sofa, making faces, unaware that my mother could see her in the mirror. All of a sudden, my mother's shoe went sailing across the room. It barely missed my oldest sister's head. It went through the double paned window. We found the shoe the next morning in the middle of the street. If it had hit its target, there would have been some serious damage.

The funny thing about this incident was that my sister saw the shoe coming but refused to duck. Her defiance made her face look like a stuffed bull frog. Now, my mother is raging mad! She had broken two window panes and my oldest sister seemingly had not even blinked an eye. She was made to clean up the glass and it appeared as though her face and eyes kept bulging. My other sister and I were too afraid to say a word until my mother left the room. Then, my sister used this opportunity to taunt the "bull frog" until we heard our mother coming back.

The saga continued the next day by escalating into a fight between my sisters. I'd never seen so much violence in all of my eight years! First, my oldest sister breaks a blood vessel in my nose. Next, my mother tries to disfigure my oldest sister's face with a shoe. Then to make things worse, my sisters were going for blood with each other. They had begun arguing about who was going to carry a bag of laundry to my aunt's house. They fought and when it was over, my oldest sister had bitten my other sister in the face. My other sister has bitten my oldest sister's finger. These bites were very serious and left scars for a very long time. This final event left me terrified. I didn't know what to think and you can believe that I definitely did not say one word! It was a terrible sight. We still went to do the laundry and all of us were walking down the street looking as though we had just left a funeral. None of us said anything to the other and each of us had tears in our eyes. It appeared that my oldest sister was still angry about the prior events of the day before. I think that she was scared because she didn't know what my mother was going to do when she came home from work. For the love of me, I can't remember what happened that evening after my mother found out about the fight.

Years later, we found ourselves laughing about this too – one sister eating bull frog and the other eating finger sandwiches. My sister would tell my oldest sister that she should have never even thought of lifting a finger to her considering all the times that she had protected her. When they were younger, my oldest sister was afraid to fight. It was a known fact among their peers in North Carolina, that if you bothered the oldest sister, her younger sister would take care of the offender, whether it be male or female. It was noted that my oldest sister had "a lot of bark but no bite" while the other sister would not leave room for much discussion before she would pounce on someone.

All of our disasters did not include violence. In fact, in all of our years together until the time that we became adults, those were the only incidences that I can recall fighting between us. However, there were times that we would get into other negative situations due to the fact that they had an adorable, loving baby sister who had a tendency to stray off the beaten path (life for them must have been very dull without me). Let me mention one of those incidences.

It was approximately a twelve block walk to my aunt's house. Our routine route would take us pass a store-front church that was the center of attention on 7th Street, NW. Sometimes, there would be music and we would stop and try to peek in to see what was going on. Most of the time, we would be met at the door by someone, with a stern look, to make us leave. We were not allowed to go in. When we told our mother about the church, she instructed us to never go in. Still, we would occasionally try to peek in. This was not too difficult during the warm or hot months.

One Sunday afternoon we stopped by that church to peek in and something was unusual. We heard the people clapping and singing and the music was much more than we had ever heard before. I needed to know what was going on. Despite the fact that we had been turned away many times and despite the warning that we received from my mother, I opened the door and walked right in. I did it so fast that my sisters couldn't stop me! I imagine that the ushers only allowed them to come in so that we would not cause a disturbance. She sternly warned us to keep quiet and to keep still – "don't move from this seat."

What we observed was really interesting. There was a man, dressed in a white suit, sitting on a very large wicker chair that looked like a throne. He had very long hair and long fingernails. If memory serves me correctly, I believe that his nails were painted red, white, and blue. There was a woman, also dressed in white, standing on each side of the chair. Each had a very large and long white feather that they used to fan the man. Everybody in the church (except me and my sisters) was dressed in white. Many people took turns in getting up and saying something about this man that they called "daddy." Some would read from a book (I don't know whether or not it was a Bible) or they would sing and play music.

Suddenly things took a turn and it became increasingly funny. There were some young children who came in to "dance for daddy." They were followed by older children who also danced. After the children had completed their dancing, some adult women came to "dance before daddy." Then "daddy" got up to say something and when he finished, he instructed everybody to dance. By this time, my sisters and I had been silenced for the second time. Then it happened! When everybody started to dance, and I do mean dance (some were almost coming out of their clothes, sweating and wiggling in front of "daddy'), I literally reeled with laughter. I almost fell off of the seat! My sisters were trying to stop me but they soon joined in with me. When the usher notice us mocking and laughing, she stopped dancing and come over to usher us out the door. I was still throwing my arms in the air and laughing when we got outside. (Even as I am writing about this event, I am laughing out loud with tears running from my eyes).

It was not until the following day that I realized that we were in "Daddy" Grace's church – The House of Prayer. During the lunch recess at school, I was telling some of my classmates about the experience. While everyone else was laughing, I noticed that there was one girl, leaning on the wall watching us. She didn't say anything at the time, but when we were going back into the building after lunch, she stopped me. She showed me a little pocket knife and said that if she ever heard me talking about "daddy" again, she would scratch my face up. She also told me that if I said anything to the teacher, she would have her brothers beat me up. Just think – I could have been scarred for life because of my disrespect for "daddy." **But God!!** My heavenly Father protected me. You can believe that, after that encounter, whenever I had anything to say about "daddy", it was strictly between me and my sisters. The events of that Sunday afternoon became our secret for a very long time. The House of Prayer remains in that same location almost sixty years later. It is no longer a store front, but a monumental and beautiful edifice (both inside and out). We never went back to that store front. However, I did attend a funeral in the new edifice a few years ago.

When I think back on that event now, I am beginning to wonder if that girl may have sent her brothers after me anyway. I didn't know her or her brothers. However, a few weeks after the incident, there were two boys at the school, who began teasing and threatening me almost every day. First off, they would follow me home, calling me names. After about a week, they began hitting me. It got to the point that I would run home from school every day. If they caught me, they would hit me. Most of the time, they didn't catch me before I got inside the gate to my house. They would never come into the yard.

My mother put an end to the chasing, although not in a manner that you would expect a mother to protect her child. One day she was looking out of the window and saw those boys chasing me. It sounded as though it was not the first time that she had seen them. She said that if she ever saw me running from them again, she would whip me herself. I would have rather tangled with a mad dog than to have to face that strap. The very next day, I waited until I saw those boys and I didn't run. I walked up to them and informed them that my mother saw them chasing me and said that she had better not see it again. Of course, I didn't tell them that the threat was directed toward me and not them. I had no more trouble out of them.

My mother had no idea of what she started with that one comment. From that point, no matter how afraid I might have been, I became a verbal warrior. As the old folk put it, I sold "wolf tickets." As the years went by, I would not only sell the ticket, I would back it up when necessary (male or female). You win some and you lose some. I didn't lose many. When I did lose, it was because the odds were stacked against me according to size. I was extremely skinny, but I would not back down. I didn't mind getting beat as long as I could get in a good punch.

Almost to her dying days, my mother never missed an opportunity to tell any and every one about how I would fight. She would tell her version this way: "You could always tell when there was about to be a fight in the neighborhood. The kids would come knocking, all excited and calling for her to hurry and come out." My only defense to her story was: "You started it when you said that you would beat me if you caught me running from anyone." She would laugh and accuse me of taking it to the extreme. I would laugh as I silently accused her of enjoying the fight in me.

I suppose that one would say that I was developing as a normal person. Well, that remains to be seen. Even at this very early stage of my life, I could have become another story with a tragic end. **But God!!** I didn't have a clue about the greatness of God then. Now, I can only imagine that throughout the years, in spite of what was happening, He would look at me and say, "For I know the thoughts that I think toward you…thoughts of peace and not of evil, **to give you a future and a hope** (Jeremiah 29:11).

"The events of childhood do not pass, but repeat themselves
like seasons of the year."
Eleanor Farjeon (1881 – 1965)
English author of children's stories

CHAPTER FIVE:
Continuing Education
And Development

The next few years of my life were not very eventful. However, there were events that stand out in my memory. My continuing education and development did not have a lot to do with school. I recall that my development was more of a mental nature, i.e. the way that I responded to things that I learned in general. We moved quite often but for the most part, things were pretty much routine. As I start this chapter, I am still eight years old and in the third grade. I was no longer impressed with school and my ability to learn. There were some good experiences and some not so good.

In the third grade, I realized that I needed to know more than the three "R's." It was during that school year that we began learning about current events. Most current events had to do with the possibility of our country being involved in wars. These lessons included the introduction to war bonds. The children were asked to bring ten cents every week to help our school purchase war bonds. It was our patriotic duty.

In addition, we would have regular "bomb drills" so that we would be prepared in the event that we came under attack. I thought that it was stupid for us to have to go to the basement and crawl under desks - "just in case." However, I did not complain because I remembered that when I lived with my grandmother, I thought the same thing when there was a thunder storm. Mama said that when it thundered, God was talking and when God talks, we had to be quiet and keep still. I recall one of those storms. As usual, mama made me sit in the corner and I wasn't too happy because I wanted to play. I thought to myself, "Why do I always have to sit in the corner? Nothing is going to happen." Almost on cue, there was a loud clap of thunder and a loud rumble on the roof. The house seemed to shake (probably my imagination). I was scared speechless and could not move. Later, when the storm was over, mama said that lightning had hit the chimney and the noise was bricks falling off of the roof. There were quite a few bricks in the back yard. The memory of that event always came to mind during the bomb drills. I would tell myself, "Just do what they tell you."

When I was ten years old, I spent the summer in North Carolina with my grandmother. By this time, mama had married my biological grandfather and had moved to his house. "Gramps" was really nice but something about mama had changed. She was quiet most of the time and gramps did most of the cooking and cleaning.

Gramps had a black horse that was so beautiful, that I would spend time everyday just watching him. I never saw Gramps ride him (he said that he was too old to ride), I think Gramps did not ride because he had a bad leg. One day, Gramps decided to give me the horse. I was really excited until I found out that I had to feed it. I then discovered that I was afraid of it. Those big yellow teeth looked like they could take my hand off. I was so afraid that no amount of coaxing from Gramps could make me feed that horse. So, I gave him back. In exchange for the horse, Gramps gave me some brand new baby chicks. Those I could handle as long as I didn't have to go near the rooster. That bird was so mean, nobody could go near him but Gramps. Unlike the other chickens, the rooster had to be fenced in at all times.

Mama didn't seem to be doing well, so they sent me to spend the last two to three weeks with her sister. Gramps crated up the chicks and I took them with me. I had fun watching them grow and taking care of them. That's when I found out that chickens could fly. As they grew, they began to roost in the trees.

There was not much to do at my aunt's house. Fortunately, she did have television that we could watch in the evenings. As for days – BORING! The things that I did as a four or five year old no longer worked for me. I would sit on the porch with nothing to do but blow bubbles with a mixture that I made from soap scraps. I use an empty spool as my blower. Sometimes, I would help my aunt in the garden and it was my responsibility to take care of the chicks. One day, I decided to climb up the plum tree to get some of the new plums. My aunt had told me not to climb the tree the first time she saw me trying. Well, I had to do something besides just sit around. So, I climbed the tree. Just as I reached to pull a plum, I saw a snake. I immediately dropped to the ground, not even thinking that I could get hurt. I did hurt my ankle, but no matter – better that than a snake bite. I managed to get back to the porch and I just sat there with my heart feeling like it was going to burst through my chest. I don't know how long I had been sitting there when my aunt came to see what I was doing. She knew immediately. She asked me why I was so quiet. Then she answered her own question. "Oh," she said, "You've been in the tree. I see it in your eyes. You saw a snake didn't you?" She told me later that she knew because my eyes were "blood shot." Needless to say, the plums on the ground suddenly became better than the ones on the tree. Even so, I was reluctant to go near the tree again.

The day before I was to come back home, my aunt killed two of the chicks for my lunch. I was upset and didn't want them, but my aunt told me that it would be chicken or nothing. On the train ride back, it didn't take long for me to get hungry enough to eat them.

Home Again

I arrived back in DC and was met by my uncle – the one with the secrets. He didn't get much of an opportunity to get me alone anymore so it had been a long time since he had "played" with me. Well, we were alone and he tried but I told him that I didn't like it. He didn't get a chance to do anything because he was driving and I wouldn't let him touch me. The next day, my mother asked me if he had ever touched me in my private area. I told her no because, by then, I was definitely sure that what he was doing was wrong. I didn't know what to expect from my mother if I had told her the truth. She questioned me a little more and told me if he ever tried to touch me, I should let her know immediately. She also told me why she was asking me about him. Apparently, he had been touching some of my older cousins and they had finally told their parents. I didn't know what to say, so I said nothing.

What I was thinking was another matter. I was mad and hurt. All those years that he had me thinking that I was the only one with whom he shared secrets. All the times that I wanted to tell and didn't. I was old enough to begin to realize the injury of lying and I felt the pain. As my grandmother would say, he was "making a fool of me" and I didn't like it one bit!

Later, I was very glad. The next time that he tried to touch me was his last. I told him that my mother had told me about him touching my cousins. I also told him that if he ever touched me again, I would tell my mother and anybody else who asked. I was glad that I wouldn't have to worry about that secret anymore. Little did I know that there were worse secrets that I would have to endure.

My oldest sister had gotten married while I was on summer vacation. She was still living with us because her husband was in the army. We moved again and things were going well until I became the "victim" of my mother's past. The teacher had given the class forms to fill out. Where it asked for my mother's maiden name, I put her name as it was at the time. My teacher told me to come back and correct it. I told her that it was correct and she insisted that I was wrong (all of this conversation was before the entire class). She asked me to explain what maiden name meant and I did. She then asked, "If maiden name means before marriage, how can your mother's maiden name be the same as her current name?" I told her that my mother was not married. She sounded indignant as she told me that I should not tell people that my mother was not married. Then she called me to her desk to privately tell me why. I was embarrassed almost to tears.

I believe that this revelation was the catalyst for my low self-esteem. From that day forward, I felt that none of my classmates liked me or that they were whispering about me behind my back. I don't know if they withdrew or if I did. I only know that I had very few friends for the remainder of that school year. When I told my mother what had happened, she only said that the teacher should have had enough sense not to question me in front of the class. No concern that I was too embarrassed to go back to school. That embarrassment turned into being ashamed of my mother. Later, as I grew older, it turned into disrespect for her, but I couldn't dare express that emotion.

Hurricane Hazel

During that same school year, Hurricane Hazel hit the DC area. I had never heard of a hurricane before and thought it strange that we were dismissed from school because a storm was heading our way. It was about one or two o'clock in the afternoon when we were sent home with an urgent warning to go home as quickly as possible – "Do not to stop anywhere, but go directly home." As quickly as possible seemed to have taken forever. There were not many people or cars on the street. I lived approximately six blocks from school. As I started out towards home, for the first couple of blocks, I notice how unusually quiet it seemed. The wind was blowing and I felt myself being pushed by it. It started to rain lightly by the time that I was half way home. Then it appeared as though it suddenly began to get dark. I tried to pick up my pace, but the wind kept pushing me back. I was almost two blocks from home when it became difficult to control my steps. The wind was pushing me all over the place. I was getting scared. By this time, I saw only a few cars passing by. I made it another block when the wind pushed me so hard that I almost fell. From that point, it was panic. I didn't know what to do. There was no one to help me. **BUT GOD!!**

I managed to move a few more steps to the corner and while waiting for a car to pass, another gust of wind began pushing me again. I was near a lamp post and I grabbed it to keep from being pushed into the street. I wrapped both arms around the lamp post and held on for dear life. It was a struggle and I was really afraid! I had two more blocks to go and one of them was up a steep hill. I didn't know it then, but God definitely had angels protecting me. By the time that I had calmed down enough to let go of that lamp post, the wind had also calmed enough for me to start walking again. My heart was racing and I decided that my body needed to do the same. I started running. I took a short cut through the alley and it wasn't too bad until I came out on the other side. I was at the lower end of the hill and the wind seemed stronger than before. There were cars parked on the street and every time that I felt that I would fall, I stepped in between cars to brace myself. I finally made it to our apartment building by continuing up the hill and shielding myself between the cars when necessary.

No one was home when I arrived, but I had a key to get in. My heart was still racing and it took a while for me to calm down. I don't know how long it took me to get home or how long I was home alone. One of my sisters finally came home and other people that lived in the building were also coming in. Many of the neighbors gathered in the hallways to exchange stories of their ordeal of trying to get home.

Our apartment had a balcony and I stepped out to see the damage that they were talking about. There was an eerie darkness. You could tell that it was still day time but it looked like it was very late in the evening. Just as the neighbors were saying, it was raining really hard and the wind was blowing the tree limbs and objects around as though they were pieces of paper. I literally saw part of a roof being ripped off of one of the buildings. Such excitement! That thunder storm that tore the chimney off of my grandmother's house was nothing compared to this. My mother and my oldest sister didn't get home until very late that night. My oldest sister said that she had almost been hit by a falling tree.

In the days that followed, we heard about a lot of damage and lives that were lost. I looked up some of the information on that storm (while I am writing about it) and discovered that the winds in our area reached seventy-eight miles per hour with gusts up to one hundred miles per hour. I was extremely skinny for my age and could not have weighed more than seventy pounds at the time. It was no wonder that I was having a problem trying to stay on my feet. My oldest sister was pregnant at the time and trying to get home from work when a falling tree almost hit her. She said that the buses were not running and she was trying to shelter herself from some of the rain. The tree barely missed her. Eventually, someone one stopped and offered her a ride, bringing her from Maryland to DC. Our family could have been included in the reports of disaster and death – **BUT GOD!**

God is our refuge and strength, an ever-present help in trouble.
~ Psalm 46:1~
NIV

CHAPTER SIX:
Death Angels

Recalling the events of Hurricane Hazel brought back memories of other near death incidents in my family. When I go back to my earliest memories, I can't think of anyone that I knew that had died, except for my favorite uncle. He was my grandmother's brother. He lived somewhere upstate (I think Michigan) and he would visit with us when the weather was warm. I can almost see him now, although I was quite young when he died. He was very tall and had the same beautiful white hair as my grandmother. That was their only resemblance. My grandmother was dark brown skinned and his skin was much lighter, like their sister who looked like a Cherokee Indian. I have been told that both Cherokee and French Indian were included in our family bloodline. My uncle's eyes were a very light brown that seemed to light up when he smiled. He always came with a toy and He would play games with me as though he were a child. He taught me how to play checkers and Chinese checkers, we would build forts out of bottle tops, and I could look forward to an ice cream cone and a quarter before he went back home. When he died, his body was brought back to North Carolina. I remember going to the church and to the cemetery. I did not understand why they put him in the ground and threw dirt on him. My oldest sister almost fell in with him. I don't know how, I just remember someone screaming and a man grabbing her by the dress as she was falling. I now believe that she could have been killed if she had fallen into that hole. **BUT GOD!!**

My first minute understanding of death came when my brother became very ill. Prior to that, I would hear people talking about someone that had died, but it didn't mean much until I hear my mother talking about my brother. My brother was about three years old at the time. He had a severe case of asthma. He would catch a cold at the least exposure to rain or severe weather. We were always warned to get him in the house if it started to rain. One weekend, he didn't come to stay with us and we were told that he was in the hospital. I heard my mother telling someone that he was unconscious and the doctors weren't giving much hope. After a few days, she said that he was awake, but the doctors still were not giving much hope. He had had an asthma attack which was complicated by pneumonia. However, he did start to get better and I believe that he was home within about a week. He almost died – **BUT GOD!!**

The next year, it was my mother that became very ill. I woke up one morning and my mother was not at home. My sisters told me that she was sick and in the hospital. My sisters had to take care of me. Every day, they would make sure that I was ready for school. One of the mothers of the church would come by every day to make sure that everything was in order.

On Sundays, my sisters would go to the hospital to visit my mother. They would leave me in the lobby of the hospital because I was not old enough to visit. When they were ready to leave, they would sneak me up to the door to see my mother and let me wave at her. I think that it took about three Sundays before I decided that I wouldn't settle for waving. It was on Easter Sunday and the mother of the church had bought me a beautiful yellow dress. I was so happy about my dress that I just had to let my mother see it. We went to the hospital and my sisters left me downstairs as usual. By this time, I had learned how to find my way to my mother's ward. I went upstairs and opened the door. When the nurse would not let me come in, I did something that I'd never done in my nine years – I threw a tantrum (although I didn't know that that was what it was called then). I screamed, jumped, kicked, and fell on the floor. Falling on the floor was an accident. I surely didn't want to mess up my pretty dress. The nurse called for reinforcement. The other nurse, who came to help, decided that it would be best to allow me a short visit because I was disturbing the other patients on the ward.

I was so happy that I could see my mother. Then, I wasn't so happy. Her arms were black and blue (bruises from needles, I was told) and she was too weak to sit up. She patted me, told me I was very pretty and gave me a big smile. They got me to leave by telling me that she needed to rest so that she could get better. I don't remember how long she was in the hospital, but I know that it was a very long time. I don't know what was wrong. However, based on later conversations, I do know that she, too, almost died. First me (when I lived in New York), then my brother, then my mother - **BUT GOD!!**

Death became a frightening thought. But God spared us! I believe that He was still saying to Himself, "I know the plans that I have for you." He has proven Himself to be bigger than our greatest situations in life, including the threats of death.

A friend is a brother who was once a bother.
~ Author unknown ~

CHAPTER SEVEN:
My Little Brother

Except for the time when my brother almost died, I have not said much about him. I think that I had a love-hate relationship with him. One minute I loved him. Within a very short period of time, I could hardly wait until he went back home to his grandmother. I didn't really hate him, I just found him to be irritating at times. The real truth about my feelings – I was jealous of him. He seemed to get all of the attention when he came to stay with us on the weekends. I didn't care that he was just a baby. I didn't think that it was fair that he could do anything that I did and not get in trouble. I would get scolded because I was supposed to know better. Maybe so, but this little boy was smart and knew how to get what he wanted. Sometimes, he knew that I would be the one to get in trouble.

Allow me to go back to when he was three years old; around the time of his brush with death. First, let me take this opportunity to say, "Thank You God!" Not only did he not die, his asthma attacks became fewer and less severe. Within two to three years, he stopped having asthma attacks. He tells me that he can't remember being a sick child.

His grandmother attributed the change in his health to the fact that he was crazy about Ovaltine. He had to have his chocolate milk at least three times a day. I didn't really like it and the only time that I drank it was on the few occasions that I spent the night with him at his grandmother's house. It was on one of those visits that I found out why I didn't like Ovaltine. His grandmother had a secret formula. She was adding raw egg to the mixture. She would never prepare the Ovaltine when he was in the house. She had to let me in on the secret when she was feeling sick and needed me to mix it. She sent my brother out to play with his friend and asked me to stay and help her "do something." Well, brother dear, if you didn't already know, the secret is out now.

My brother was really smart for his age. It didn't take long for him to learn anything. He could see a car from a block away and tell you what kind of car it was. He was making speeches at our church activities when he was three or four years old. The only time that I can recall him ever forgetting his lines was when he became distracted by an urgent need to empty his bladder. He made a hasty exit with the announcement of what he was going to do. He was the youngest in the Junior Choir and always learned the songs before most of the others.

My brother also had a passionate love for money. He could count money as well as I could and would always try to save it. Keep in mind that I'm still talking about when he was three or four years old. Sometimes, on the weekend, my aunt or mother would give us a nickel or dime. A dime went a long way. One Saturday, we each had a dime. My brother tricked me into spending my money to buy us a cupcake. He told me that he would buy us a Popsicle later. After eating his cupcake, he put his money in his bank and refused to buy the Popsicle. Therefore, I decided to take back my money. He ran to tell my mother that I was taking HIS money! Now, you know that I was mad. Not only had I let my little brother trick me, my mother wouldn't let me get my money back.

Now, if I don't tell you this, my brother will never forgive me. We can never reminisce without him bringing up his favorite memory. When he would visit on the weekend, my sisters were responsible for taking him back home on

Monday morning. They did this for a while but when he turned four years old, they would put him on the streetcar and told the conductor where to let him off. From the point of discharge, he would have to cross a very busy intersection and walk home alone. When they were satisfied that he could do this, the responsibility was passed off to me. He was so proud of the fact that he could go home by himself that, per instructions from my sisters, he didn't tell his grandmother. My sisters and I would split the twenty cents that we saved by not riding the streetcar with him.

When we moved to the apartment on the hill, we took turns walking him home. As soon as I learned the way (about the same time as he did), I had to take him home every Monday. After a short period of time, I started walking him part of the way and would allow him to go the remainder by himself. Each week, the distance that I went with him became shorter and shorter. I would leave him at a certain point and go back home. One morning his grandmother decided to meet us and our little secret was over. She called my mother to inform her that my brother was being sent home alone. This led to the discovery of how long we had been sending him home alone. Once again, I found myself in big trouble. I had a problem with being the only one who was punished even though my sisters told me to do it.

My brother's "security blanket" was actually a monkey made out of socks. He carried that monkey everywhere but to church. When it was time for the monkey to be washed, he was very anxious until he got it back. Sometimes, I would hide it from him and tease him. I don't remember how he got over needing that monkey, but somewhere in the back of my mind, I think that I dropped it over my friend's balcony. She lived on the back side of our building and it was impossible to get up the hill to retrieve it. It was irreplaceable because my mother's employer had made it for him. Well, he was almost seven and finally got over it.

As I got older, I became more jealous. My brother had his father and I didn't have one. There was money for him to take piano lessons, but there was none for me to become a girl scout. He made his parents proud. I was becoming a problem. The last negative event that I recall between us was when I was approximately twelve years old. I don't remember the details except that we were arguing and the argument ended up with us fighting (nothing serious, just a couple of licks between us). My mother made us both go to bed. I felt like I was being punished for something that he started. I was so furious that I stated hitting myself because I wanted to hit him and knew that it would be more trouble for me if I did. So I inflicted the pain that was intended for him on me. I said something negative with every blow that I directed to my head, i.e., "I wish I was dead. I hate him. He gets away with everything. Nobody cares about me." I hit myself so hard that I ran out of energy. Then I hung my head off of the side of the bed and my nose began to bleed.

My brother called my mother to tell her that I was bleeding. When he told her how it happened, she calmly cleaned me up and then beat me. She said that if I wanted to beat myself to death, she would help me get started again. She only gave me a couple of licks on the backside and they didn't hurt my body but my feelings were hurt. I was seething and at that moment, my rage was internalized and turned to hate. I hated my mother. I didn't want my brother to say anything to me and I wouldn't talk to him. I think the sight of the blood scared him a little and I was happy about that. He sat on his bed for a long time, watching me until he fell asleep. As for me, this incident was more fuel for my low self-esteem. Nobody liked me and I was hurt!

I realize that this chapter could have ended another way. I see too many families feuding over things that happened when they were children. They continue to fuss and cuss each other or even worse, have nothing at all to do with each other. **BUT GOD!!**

I can honestly say that I love my brother dearly, and I know that he loves me. He thinks that I'm one of the strongest women that he has ever known. He tells me that he is proud to have me as his sister. I've given him his own space in my story because I am so proud of his accomplishments and I really do love him. No more jealousy. As adults, we have sat down and told each other how we envied each other as children. Neither of us ever knew how the other felt until we talked about it a few years ago. I wanted a father. He wanted to live with his mother and sisters. Nonetheless, we survived. Love covers a multitude of faults. We are the only two of my mother's children that remain. I can say without a doubt that we are glad to have each other. The devil was scheming against us – **BUT GOD!!**

I sink deep in mire, where there is no standing: I am come
into deep waters, where the floods overflow me.
~ Psalm 69:2 ~

CHAPTER EIGHT:
Life Goes Down Hill

When that last incident with my brother happened, we were no longer living in the apartment on the hill. We were now caretakers in an apartment building in the Adams-Morgan area. At that time, the only black homeowners, living in the community, were confined to one block. The other blacks were caretakers and lived in the janitor's quarters of apartment buildings. We moved into the building during the summer before I started junior high school. My oldest sister had move to her own apartment when her husband came home from the army.

The laws of desegregation were being enforced at that time. Therefore, I was among the first black students (there were twelve of us) to integrate Gordon Junior High School in Georgetown. We were not bussed to school; we had to use public transportation. It took almost an hour of travel time. The rules, regarding acceptable behavior were laid out the first day. The number one rule was that absolutely no fighting would be tolerated. None of us blacks seemed to mind being in a white school and eventually many of the whites were okay with it. However, it was evident that some of the teachers had problems with us being there. I remember that one of the teachers blatantly told us that colored people didn't belong in that school. She was old and did whatever she could to provoke us. Stay tuned for more about her.

Change Was Not Easy

Junior high school was a lot different than what I was accustomed to. However, I had no problem with making the necessary adjustments. My problem was with making adjustments at home. There were major changes. When we moved to our new apartment (janitor's quarters), my life took a downward spiral. My sister and I had chores that made us look like Cinderella. We didn't complain much. We understood that the building had to be kept clean and that all of us had to help. The only thing that bothered me was that my friends, who also lived in janitor's quarters, seldom had to help their parents clean the buildings. They were only required to help out in their living quarters.

I felt like I was being deprived of my childhood. I didn't get to hang out much with my friends. My mother was still working outside of the home. Therefore, my sister and I had to do a great portion of the chores to keep the building clean.

My typical week was as follows: Monday through Friday, I had to get up early enough to pull thrash from four floors (no elevators, approximately eight apartments per floor). I would then have to go back up and sweep the floors and stairways. I had to leave home at eight o'clock and was generally back home around four or four-thirty. I did whatever chores my mother had assigned for our personal space and then homework. If time allowed, I would go out with my friends. I had to be home when it started to get dark. On Saturdays, I did the trash and sweeping routine. Added to that was the gruesome toil of mopping those hallways and cleaning the banisters. The banisters were made of wrought iron with intricate designs. It took a couple of hours to wipe every area of those banisters. After finishing the hallways and banisters, I had to clean the glass entrance doors to the building and polish the gold chrome around the doors and the address plates. If there were any vacant apartments in the building, we would have to clean and get them ready for rental. Cleaning the apartments included sanding and shellacking the floors by hand. That's right – no sanding machines – on our hands and knees with steel wool pads and varnish. If I had any energy left, I could hang out on Saturday afternoons and Sundays, after church. The apartments also had to be painted. I don't remember who did that.

Shortly after moving into our apartment, we moved next door. Now, we had two buildings to keep clean. Our personal living area was larger than the first and kept as clean as the tenant apartments. Our apartment was immediately next to the furnace room. The furnace was fueled by coal. To get an idea of how clean our area was, my mother hung our laundry in the open area next to the furnace room. That basement was cleaner than any of the other basements in which my friends lived. To some, this may sound like a form of violation of the child labor law, but it was nothing compared to the things that followed.

Shortly after we moved into the second apartment, I found out that my sister was pregnant. Therefore, as time went by, I had to do more work. After she had the baby, she got a job. Sometimes, I would idolize my sister. She had an eye for nice things, especially clothes. I called her my "Eartha Kitt" or "Carman Jones." I thought that she looked so good that if I saw her coming down the street, I would stop whatever I was doing just to watch her. When she went out, she would "dress to the nines." Sack dresses, chemises, and fish tail dresses were the styles. She wore them well, mostly with bareback shoes. I would tell myself that I would look just like her when I grew up. Later – some thirty years later – my sister had turned into my mother, as far as looks were concerned. In her later years, she was obviously overweight and fashions didn't mean much to her any more. She still had an eye for nice things. She spent her money on nice household items and bought her children the best. We often laughed at the idea that I had wanted to look just like her – shapely in all the right places. I thanked God, often, that He didn't grant me that wish.

At thirteen, I did not like myself much. My friends were starting to blossom and I became "Skinny Minnie" and "Boney Maroney." Embarrassing! My self-esteem, or lack of it, made me afraid to say or do anything that would draw attention to myself. Then, I discovered that attention could be good. I became the "clown" or the "wolf", whichever was necessary. I liked to act silly. It helped me to relax. I liked to act tough. It kept me from having to fight unless absolutely necessary. How in the world did my mother get the idea that I was the ringleader when it came to fighting? I was only protecting myself.

Thirteen brought about some other changes for which I was not ready. I, like all of my girlfriends, was starting to like boys. We would spend our free time playing ball on a vacant lot or going to each other's houses (except mine) to listen to music and dance. When we were not with the boys, the girls would spend our time talking about them – which one was the nicest or the cutest, etc. We would spend our money on Rhythm and Blues magazines or the latest hit records. "Forty-fives" were the newest records on the market at that time.

It was during this phase of my life that I developed a profound love for reading. Since I was home long before most of my friends, I spent most of my evenings reading comic books, mysteries, and magazines, such as True Story, True Confessions and others books that claimed that the love stories were from real life experiences. By the time that my mother found out that I was reading the "forbidden" magazines, I was hooked. She forbade me to read them and tore up the ones that I had. I would only buy more and hide them somewhere. I figured that those books gave me some much needed education regarding sex. The only other education that I received on that topic was a documentary shown at school concerning the reproductive cycle and a wealth of information from my mother, which consisted entirely of five words – "Keep your skirt tails down." On the other hand, the magazines taught me the principles of no sex before marriage and the consequences to be faced if I did engage in sexual activity before marriage. Well, a lot of good that did me. Regardless of how much I thought that I knew, I still got caught up into it with devastating consequences.

I remember my "first love." He lived around the corner from me. His parents were homeowners. He was really nice and easy going. He was well liked by all of us, male and female. I had kissed a few boys before, but the first kiss with him was different. With the others, it was like grab, kiss and see what else I can get. With him, it was like take your time and enjoy the trip. Trust me – I enjoyed the trip! I really liked him a lot. He started coming to my house and we would sit outside for hours just talking and sometimes holding hands. Our friends began teasing us but we didn't care. One night, he and another friend came to see me and one of my girlfriends. We talked for a while and the boys convinced us to go for a walk with them. I knew that I would get in trouble if my mother found out that I had left from in front of the apartment. I didn't care and I went. Long story short, we ended up in a compromising position and I was scared half to death. I wanted what he wanted but I was afraid. I backed off at the last minute. Needless to say, he was not too happy, especially since his buddy had scored with my friend. He didn't come by the next evening. A couple of days later, we talked. He assured me that I would not get pregnant because he "used protection." He even showed it to me. I told him that I couldn't and he said, "Okay." Two day later, he was talking with the new girl in the neighborhood. I was devastated when he was honest enough to tell me that he liked me but he needed something more than a kiss every now and then. To make matters worse, none of the girls that were my friends, wanted to be friends with the new girl. She was overweight and unattractive. I was the only one that would befriend her. Now, she had my boyfriend because she was willing to do what I wouldn't. Let's pour a little salt into that injury; she shared the news of her "new found love" with me, not knowing that he was my boyfriend. I really wanted to tell her that he only wanted her body, but why break her heart? What was I to gain from that? Even if I had been willing to put out, the chances of me and my boyfriend getting together would have been almost impossible. My mother said that I was too young to have a boyfriend. This girl was having sex at home with her mother in the next room. AND, her mother knew it! How was I supposed to compete with that? The magazines were right – they only want you for your body!

There's a Dog in the House!

My resentment and embarrassment regarding my mother was increasing. A new school and new neighborhood did not change the fact that my mother was not married. To make matters worse, I had to correct my friends' assumption that the man in the house was my father. My mother's boyfriend was there most of the time – night and day. In the beginning, he would go home late at night but gradually, he started to spend the night more often.

A few days after my breakup with my boyfriend, I got the shock of my life. I came home early and found my sister and my mother's boyfriend – caught in very act! I was so stunned that I just stood there staring in disbelief. He rushed into the next room. My sister appeared to be paralyzed. When she could finally say something, it was, "If you tell, I'll tell mother that you were doing the same thing with your boyfriend." I tried to explain that we were only kissing, but she insisted that she would tell my mother that I was having sex. Can you believe?? As much as I wanted to, and didn't, I was accused anyway. I decided not to tell. I didn't say anything to anybody. However, I made a decision at that point. The next time I wanted to have sex, I would! If my boyfriend hadn't already gotten with someone else, I would have gone looking for him with the sole purpose of "giving it up."

At this point, I liked my mother even less. My respect for her was almost completely down the drain. She was just like some of the women that I read about in the magazines. How dare she tell me no sex when she was sleeping with someone that was not her husband? The man was no good!!

How could she do this? Let me tell you a little more about this man. Fasten your seat belt!

When I came to live with my mother and sisters, he was in the picture. We didn't see him very often. He would occasionally come by our house to pick up my mother. In the summer time, he would take us all to the waterfront, at night, in an effort to help us cool off from the sweltering heat. He never came into our house until we moved into the janitor's quarters. I once heard my mother telling someone that they were not married, due to a prior relationship on his part. The story was that he had been falsely imprisoned for murder. His family turned on him and his girlfriend seemingly was the only one who stuck by him during the trial and all the years that he spent in prison. When he was released (after it was determined that he had not committed murder, but was actually defending himself), he was alienated from most of his family. His brother brought him to DC so that he could get a fresh start. My mother met him through his brother and they became friends. They had been involved for more than a year before she found out about the prior girlfriend.

When he got his first rooming house, the girlfriend moved to DC to be with him. He told my mother that he was not in love with the woman, but he could never marry anyone else as long as she was living. He felt that it was his duty to take care of her. I don't know how the other woman found out about my mother, but it appeared that she accepted the fact that the man was not in love with her. My mother and this woman were sharing this man and neither of them seemed to have a problem with it. He gave this woman a nice home to live in and took care of her.

When we moved to the Adams-Morgan apartment, I became acquainted with the other woman. She would call our house if she needed to contact the boyfriend and my mother would call her for the same purpose. This woman was running a rooming house for him and he was "keeping a roof over our heads" by becoming the janitor for the two buildings that we serviced. This woman and my mother were so at ease with each other that you would have thought that they were friends. I went to her house on a few occasions and she was always very nice to me. My mother even allowed her to take me on a weekend trip to her hometown.

The man, on the other hand, was a dog! My sister was not the first. When we moved to the larger apartment building, he moved two sisters, who had been living in one of his rooming houses, into the smaller apartment so that they could help out. One sister was an alcoholic. She was as nice as you would want to see until she had too much to drink. They had only been in the apartment a few months when the alcoholic started causing trouble. She would get drunk and start an argument with anybody. One day she started an argument with my mother. She told my mother that she (my mother) was a "nobody" who couldn't keep her man and that she (the alcoholic) had been sleeping (she used the "f" word) with my mother's boyfriend. My mother quietly told her to go home and to leave her alone. (I think that I have already mentioned that my mother can be dangerous when she gets quiet during unpleasant encounters. Remember the shoe that she threw at my sister's head?) The alcoholic left but not before she reiterated that she had been sleeping with my mother's boyfriend. Shortly after the woman left, I saw my mother pick up a screwdriver and leave. I followed her into the other apartment building and hid behind a pillar and listened as my mother demanded that the woman open the door. The woman was saying all kinds of nasty things to my mother. My mother had stopping saying anything – I think that she had started "working on the lock" with the screwdriver. She must have spotted me from the corner of her eye. She told me to go home. I left and went to the other side of the building so that I could see through the window. I heard my mother tell the woman that she could come out or she would come in. That crazy woman had no better sense than to tell her to come in and get the man out of her bed (or something to that effect). With one or two slams from my mother's hand, the door was almost off of the hinges. The woman ran out so fast that I still cannot figure out how she got by my mother. I don't know what happened after that because I saw my mother walking towards the exit and I knew that I had to get back in our apartment before she did. When my mother finally came in, she was, as they say, as cool as a cucumber.

I don't know if my mother's boyfriend was sleeping with the woman or not. However, I do know that when my mother was not at home, he would spend hours in the other building before coming to our apartment. He finally evicted her and her sister. I think that the tenants started to complain about the disturbances that she caused when she was drunk.

The Dog Made His Move

The eviction, of the sisters, turned out to be too bad for me. Shortly after they moved, my mother's boyfriend told her that I was slipping out to see the boys. That was absolutely not true! Sometimes, I would sit on the wall in front of our apartment building (as I always did when I could not leave the building). I would stay outside as long as I could, in hopes that some of my friends would come by and spend some time with me. Nonetheless, my mother decided that I would have to come in when it got dark.

It wasn't long before the "dog" made his move. It was on a weekend and no one was home except me and my brother. My mother was at work. My sister had moved out. (It was years before I knew that she had moved into one of the rooming houses.) The dog came in and started doing something in my mother's room. Then he asked if my brother and I wanted some cake and Kool-Aid. Does a kid like cake and Kool-Aid? Of course, we wanted some. Well, it turned out that the Kool-Aid was spiked. My brother and I were playing a card game and we drank plenty of Kool-Aid. When he got too sleepy to play, the dog told him to take a bath and go to bed. Actually, I was sleepy too. He told me to get the bed ready for my brother. When I got up from the table, I was light-headed. I stumbled to the bed and he grabbed me, offering to "help." He started pulling at my clothes and I was too out of it to stop him. I knew what he was doing, but still could not muster up enough energy to protest. I can still remember him telling me to lay still and he would go and help my brother.

I was trying to get up when he came back into the room. He had his way with me without much of a struggle. I saw my brother come crawling into the room, obviously as out of it as I was. He was laughing, pointing, and saying, "I see you." The dog threatened to beat my brother if he didn't leave the room. He left but came back still laughing. The dog cursed and took my brother out of the room. By the time that he came back, I was really sick. It was not so much because of the Kool-Aid, it was the realization of what had just happened. I don't remember how I got to my own bed or how my brother got to his bed, which was in my mother's room – the same bed where the assault took place.

The next morning was unclear. I can't seem to remember anything about that day. I know that it had to be Sunday, but I don't know if we went to church. That day appears to be a complete blank in my mind. To make matters worse, I don't recall what was said to keep me from telling my mother what had happened. The molestation continued until I left home, two or three years later. In the meanwhile, whenever I was home alone, the dog had his way with me whenever he felt like it.

After my mother's death, my sister and I finally talked about her and the dog. She told me that he had threatened to put us all out if she said anything. He had her thinking that my mother could not get a place for us to live without his help. I asked why she stayed with him after she moved away from home. She said that by the time she had saved enough money to move out, she was afraid of him, that he would physically beat her if she tried to leave. She said that the last time he had beat her, she was so messed up that she couldn't leave the house for a week. When I asked why she had moved into one of his houses, she said that had he just gotten another house and made my mother believe that she was needed as the landlord. She indicated that my mother may have found out about them a couple of years later. However, she did not give any indication that she knew anything. My sister went to her grave, never knowing that the dog had bitten me too.

I know now what I didn't know then. The adversary was out to destroy me and he almost did. **BUT GOD!!** I was struck down but I was **NOT** destroyed!

There are those who rebel against the light; they do not know its ways nor abide in its paths.

~ Job 24:13 ~
(NKJV)

CHAPTER NINE:
Rebellion and Degradation

The next three years of my life became a time of metamorphosis. I had changed from being a little problem to an out of control, bitter, conniving, and lying teenager. I was angry with my mother, but I knew that I had better not show one bit of disrespect towards her. In essence, all of my rebellion only caused me more problems as I grew to literally hate her. There were times when I took no second thought about doing something that I knew would get me into trouble. Sometimes, I would convince myself that I was too smart to get caught and other times, I just didn't care if I did.

During my second year in junior high school, I started "acting out" to the fullest extent possible. Let me tell you about some of the really dumb things that I did. I'll start with the teacher that I mentioned who didn't want colored kids in the school that I attended. I had failed seventh grade math and had to repeat her class. There was another student that was in the same class with me that also failed and had to repeat the class. He was white. However, since we knew each other and were the only eighth grade students in that class, we became friends. Most of the time, we would come to class together, laughing and talking. The sight of us together would make the teacher cringe. One day, I had left him and as he was catching up from behind, he threw a piece of paper at me to get my attention. The teacher was at her usual station outside the front entrance to the classroom. When the paper fell at my side, she instructed me to pick it up. I was about to do so, but my friend had caught up to me and told her that he had thrown the paper and would pick it up. She glared at him and said, "I didn't tell you to pick it up. I told M____ (she used my last name) to pick it up. She then instructed me, again, to pick up the paper. I refused and she grabbed me by my arm. Wrong move! It became a verbal thing between us.

"Pick it up."

"Take your hands off of me."

"Not until you pick up the paper. Pick it up now!"

I jerked away from her so violently that I think it scared her a little. My classmate was standing and watching, not knowing what to do. I knew that I was in big trouble! I automatically went to the principal's office, knowing that she would be coming behind me in a few minutes. Of course, I was suspended from school.

Surprisingly, that incident was the only time that I can recall my mother defending my actions. She was already aware of the teacher's remarks from the previous year. When I explained what happened, she told the principal that the teacher should have not put her hands on me. However, she did not excuse my actions. She told me that I should have told her about the incident and allowed her to handle it.

I had another teacher who was not liked by most of the students – black or white. We had a nick-name for her. Most of the students called her "BPB." She always wore her hair in two thick braids that she pulled across the top of her head and held them in place with bobby pins. The "BPB" was an acronym for "Bobby Pin B____"). She was our commercial arithmetic teacher.

We had to do all of our assignments in ink and there could not be any signs of erasure or overwriting. She would post the best papers on the bulletin board in the back of the classroom. There was seldom more than three or four papers (A's & B's). I never did well in that class until she started talking down to the students that were getting poor grades. Although she was talking to about half of the class, it appeared to me that she would always be looking at me. One day, she called us worthless and that day, I said to myself, "I'll show you." We were to have a test the next day. I went home and spent the evening studying. On the day after the test, my paper was among those that were on the bulletin board. I had made a B. I knew that I would get a passing grade, but was surprised to see the B. When I saw it, I said, "I can't believe that Bobby Pin B____ gave me a B. I didn't know that she was standing behind me (teachers usually stand outside the front entrance to the classroom) until she said, "It just goes to show you what you can do." I was totally embarrassed. After class, I went to apologize to her. She just smirked as she dismissed me from the room.

Another school issue involved playing hooky with my friends. My mother knew about it before I got home at my regular time. The next day, all of us were in the principal's office with our parents. The principal asked us how we thought that they would not notice that half of the Negro population was missing from school on the same day. Caught! We knew that it was no use trying to convince them that we were not together.

Then, there was the time that one of the white students was overheard using some negative remarks about us. We decided to confront her after school, under the streetcar tunnel at DuPont circle. When we did, her friend ran for help. The police were there before we could scatter. My friends ran in so many different directions, that it was impossible to catch them all. I was too smart to get caught. I stood there, blending in with another group, looking like a spectator. The girl was so afraid that she wasn't sure who had approached her. When questioned about the incident, I suggested that it may have been some students from the high school.

There was another incident when a fight broke out in that same tunnel. I was late getting home and my mother punished me – not for being late, but because she thought that she had seen me somewhere that I should not have been. She refused to believe that it was not me that she saw. I refused to believe that my own mother didn't know her own child. That was just another log on the fire that fueled my hatred. I was so angry that I slipped out of the house the next night. It was Thanksgiving and I had convinced myself that I had nothing for which I should be thankful.

I walked the streets and cried. The more I walked, the more I thought. The more I thought, the angrier I became. I had no plans for running away. I just did it. It was late when the police stopped me at 14th and U Streets, N.W. They wanted to know why I was out so late, alone. I didn't have a good reason and they took me to the police precinct when I refused to tell them where I lived. The female officer, after a lot of time and questions, finally got me to admit that I had run away and didn't know where I was going. I could only assure her that I was not going back home. She informed me that I would be sent to the reform school if I didn't go home. She told me all of the bad things about that option, but I didn't care. I was adamant! I told her that I didn't care if my mother promised to treat me as if I were a queen, I was not going back.

So, there I was – a juvenile delinquent – not having a clue of what I was letting myself in for. I was so angry that I could have cared less, at that moment. The officer told me that she would have to let my mother know where I was before she could send me to the receiving home. I waited a very long time before I finally gave her the information that she needed. It was another long wait before I realized that my mother was told to come to the precinct to get me. When she arrived, I refused to go home with her. They finally gave up and sent me to the Receiving Home on Mount Olive Road in DC.

My stay at the Receiving Home was an eye opener. I wasn't as tough as I thought. The girls in that place were rough, to say the least. I knew, immediately, not to cross any of them. Most of the girls were bigger than me. I was really skinny for my age. One girl told me that I should try not to get into any arguments, but not to act as if I was afraid. Her advice was well taken until the day that they started to talk about "bull daggers" (we didn't know the term "lesbian" back in those days). One of the girls openly admitted that she was one. Except for her breasts, everything about her appeared to be boyish. As she was leaving the room, she brushed up against me while telling me what she would like to do to me. I knew that I had to stop her actions immediately or be subject to them for as long as I was there. Without hesitation, I hit her and the fight was on. Fortunately, some of the other girls grabbed her before she could render bodily harm. I ended up in isolation (for starting the fight).

While in isolation, my duty was to clean the Matron's bathroom. She sat me down and told me that she had put me in isolation to protect me – that I was no match for some of the girls. She also told me that I would be going to court and that I should try to patch things up with my mother and go home. I decided that she was right. I stayed in isolation for two days and when I was released back to the general area, there seemed to have been a difference among the girls. Most of them admired my "bravery" and wanted to be my friend. The others sided with the "bull", apparently out of fear. I spent a week in that place and was too glad to get out. When we met in court, I asked my mother if I could come home. She literally cried, asking me why I was putting her through so much trouble. I didn't bother to answer. She should have known.

Enslaved and Enraged

Things at home did not change except to get worse. I had so much work to do that I didn't get to go out much. That left me more vulnerable to the dog. I tried to stay out of my room as much as possible because that was where he always made his move. My room was next to the bathroom and he could make a quick escape if necessary.

One Saturday morning, my mother went out and came back earlier than expected. He caught me before I had gotten out of bed. He knew not to close the door to our apartment because if someone was home, only the screen door would be closed. The screen door was fastened with a hook and latch that we would slip our fingers through to open it. When my mother flipped the latch, he jumped up and ran to the bathroom, but not before warning that I had better be quiet. I started making my bed before my mother came to my room. She stood and looked around for a couple of seconds before asking why I wasn't upstairs cleaning the hallways. I told her that I had overslept and didn't wake up until I heard him (the dog) come in. She already knew that he was in the bathroom because the door was closed. She said nothing else, even though I was sure that she had heard his big bunch of keys hit the wall as he fled from my room. My thought was that she should have busted that door down like she had done when she had gone after the alcoholic. Wasn't I more important? Was she really so stupid not to have seen that I was avoiding looking up at her? My mother almost always knew when I was lying. Before I could get a lie out of my mouth, she would say, "Shut up. You're getting ready to tell a lie." Why didn't she know that I was lying then? More anger. More hate.

One day, I came home and turned on the TV. The dog came in right after I did and told me to go to my room. He kept walking and I kept trying to find something to watch on TV. He came back and hit me on my backside with a strap. "Didn't I tell you to take your a__ in the room?" I didn't say anything. I got up and started toward my room. I thought about the knife that he kept in a drawer in my mother's room. I was tempted to get it, but I knew that I was no match for him. So, I went to my room and tried to comfort myself with the idea that, one day, he would have to explain to my mother why I had attacked him with his own knife. I really toyed with that idea, planning to catch him when he was asleep.

From that point, I did start slipping out and every time that he threatened to tell my mother, I threatened to tell her about him. Needless to say, I had a little more freedom. My mother worked at a hospital in the evenings. She would always call home at a certain time. As long as I was home to answer the phone, I was okay.

One night, when I came in to get the call, she was home. I could have fainted. I tried to lie, but it didn't work. She was home early because she had accidently opened a jug of uncut ammonia and was overcome by the fumes. After being treated, the hospital gave her the rest of the evening off. She had been home a lot longer than I tried to tell her that I had been gone. My excuse for being out was that I had left my book at school and was trying to find one of my friends so that I could borrow her book and do my homework. Of course, she didn't believe me and I was grounded indefinitely. Home was like a prison and the dog was the warden. At the age of fourteen, I was trapped with no means of escape. No matter what I did, I didn't deserve to be locked in with that beast.

Learning to Cope with a Bad Situation

At the age of fifteen, I was so miserable that I decided to steal whatever pleasures I could. I became more rebellious but used conniving and manipulation as my tools. It seemed that I was constantly being punished and I had gotten to the place where it did not matter. The only place that I could go was to school and church. Occasionally, I was allowed to go to a friend's house or to the movies. I had a babysitting job on most Friday and Saturday nights. For a while, I decided to try being more obedient to my mother. I accepted the fact that I was in a prison without bars and the only way to get out was on good behavior. I would do really well for a while until something angered me. Then, I would "go off" again.

It was doing one of my "being good" cycles that I met a new friend. He lived in a nearby neighborhood and had started hanging with us. I still had to be home at a certain time, but I was allowed to stay on the front again. This friend would come by on Saturday afternoons and we would sit on the front and talk. Although it was early in the day, when he came to visit, we seldom went anywhere except, maybe to the park. He was nice, but I really didn't like him very much. I would try to leave home before he got there unless he called to say that he was on the way.

One Saturday, my mother sent me to do the grocery shopping. She was always so pleased that I could stretch a dollar as well as she could and still have good quality food. That was a natural for me. Food was my pacifier. I paid close attention to the brands that my mother preferred and learned how to pick the better cuts of meats. That was at least one thing that I did right. She never failed to let me know that she was proud of me when it came to grocery shopping.

When I returned from the store on that Saturday, I saw my friend coming from our apartment building. I immediately thought, "I'm in trouble now." I became very angry at the thought of being grounded again. I went into a "tailspin." The nerve of him going to my apartment after I had told him that my mother said that I was too young for a boyfriend? How dare he risk getting me in trouble? His response to those questions was, first to apologize and then to tell me that it worked.
"What worked?"
"I went to talk to your mother."
"What??"

He explained that he thought that if he introduced himself to my mother, she might allow him to take me to the movies. He said that she was very nice. She asked him questions (a lot of questions), i.e., where did he live? How old was he? What school did he attend? He said that they talked for almost a half hour while waiting for me to come home. She told him where I was and he was coming to meet me. I was totally floored. I couldn't think of anything else to say, so I told him that I was angry and didn't want to talk with him.

I left him standing in front of our building with a confused look on his face.

You can be sure that my mother did the "twenty-one questions" with me. I almost fainted when she said that she thought that my friend was a nice boy and had enough manners to ask if he could take me to the movies. And – check this out – he offered to give her his telephone number! Therefore, since he was so nice and had such good manners, she said that I could go to the movies with him. Then she said, "None of the other boys sitting around here ever came in to talk with her." What?? I was completely stunned. Is that all that had to happen in order for her to allow me to go the movies with a boy?? I had missed a lot of movies. When my girlfriends went to the movies, their boyfriends went with them. They all went as a group, but I didn't go because I didn't have a boyfriend. I had a "dog", but not a boyfriend, and the dog never went anywhere with me. Why would he?

So now, I can date someone that I didn't want to date. Well, if that was to be my ticket out of the house, so be it. He came by almost every Saturday, but we didn't always go to the movies. I didn't want my friends calling him my boyfriend. Sometimes we would walk around the neighborhood or go to the park. The zoo was only a couple of blocks from where I lived and we would go there often.

The time came when he wanted to kiss me. I hated kissing him. However, if my plan to be with my other friends more often was going to work, I knew that I would have to at least let him kiss me. There was another surprise – this guy was genuine. When I started acting as though I enjoyed kissing him and he could not conceal the fact that he was aroused, he would back off, apologize and leave. WOW! This, coupled with the fact that I would start arguments with him and leave him worked out well for a few months. When I left him or when he **had** to leave me, I would use the allotted time to catch up with my real boyfriend.

My plan backfired when I came home one evening and my mother informed that my friend had called. When she told him that I was supposed to be with him, he told her that he hadn't seen me in a few weeks. I told her that he was telling the truth – that we had a break up.

"So where have you been going?"

"Hanging with my friends."

"Where?"

"Mostly in the neighborhood – the ball field, Little Tavern, sometimes at the park or to the movies."

She only warned me that I had better not get into any trouble. I told her that was why we had the break up – it was becoming hard for us to be together. She got the message but gave me a look of wonderment.

After that discussion with my mother, I knew that I needed another plan. The solution fell right into my hands. I spent a lot of time at my real boyfriend's house. His mother was there most of the time, but she would occasionally go out and leave us with his little sister and brother. One day, she asked me if I would babysit for her a couple of evenings a week. I had her clear it with my mother. My mother didn't know her, so, she asked a lot of questions. When she asked me if there were any older children in the home, I was so glad that I had decided to tell her a "half-truth." I said that she had a son about my age, but he didn't like having to stay in to take care of the kids. Little did I know that my boyfriend's mother had said the same thing to my mother. She had even told my mother that she would see that I got home safely. As it turned out, most of the time, I was home by my normal deadline. Therefore, my mother didn't bother to ask how I got home if I said that I was going to babysit.

After about a month, my boyfriend's mother went out, regularly, a couple of evenings a week. She would never stay very long and was usually home by eight. My boyfriend and I had all the time that we needed if we wanted to be alone. We broke up a few months later when I found out that he was "talking to" the girl who lived across the street from him.

Soon after I broke up with my boyfriend, I suddenly became very "attractive" to the other guys in our neighborhood group. They would openly come on to me like flies to honey. It was not "will you be my girlfriend", but rather "let's go somewhere and do it." I could not believe the way some of them approached me. I soon discovered the reason. It appeared that my ex-boyfriend had let it be known that I was "putting out." What they didn't know was that I wasn't going to "put out" just for the fun of it. I didn't want that type of attachment connected with my name. We already had a couple of girls in the group that would do that and the rest of us would really talk bad about them. They would do it with anybody. But, NOT ME!! OH, NO!! The only one of them that I would have given in to was my first love, but he wasn't asking.

It was not always easy to say no and mean it. I discovered that my body was making demands that I had not noticed before. I would not allow the boys to have their way with me. However, I was getting messages from my body and I didn't know how to shut them down. I was unaware that sex could be like an addiction. So, the end result was that I did something worse than accommodating the boys. When I needed those urges to be relieved, I allowed the "dog" to relieve them. He was taking me anyway and I didn't have to worry about him telling anyone. I hated myself more and more each time that I submitted to him without wanting to claw his eyes out. Then I decided that getting relief was not enough. If I was going to do the unthinkable, I might as well enjoy it.

I must have had a sign on my back that said, "Ready and willing." Shortly after making the decision to enjoy lust, was my first encounter with an adult that I submitted to willingly. I was headed for destruction, knowing that I was doing wrong. Nonetheless, I didn't care. I was very familiar with the statement, "The wages of sin is death." I was not afraid to die. What could be worse than the hell in which I was living? I deliberately set out to follow the wrong course.

In fact, I was going to push Satan off of his throne and take his seat.

BUT GOD!! Many are the plans in a man's (or child's) heart, but it is the Lord's purpose that prevails (Proverbs 19:21).

The enemy pursues me, he crushes me to the ground; he makes me dwell in darkness like those long dead.

~ Psalm 143:3 ~
(NIV)

CHAPTER TEN:
Headed for the Pits

By the beginning of my ninth grade school year, I was sleeping around with an older man. He began talking to me during the summer vacation. He told me that he was twenty-three and I thought that he was just the right age – not too young or too old. I had reached the cross roads of boy versus man and man won with no hesitation. The man that I was seeing worked at the neighborhood gas station as a mechanic. By the time summer vacation was over, I was well known at the shop. When school started, he would take me to school. We got along very well and he did not pressure me for sex. We would hug, kiss, get all worked up and it ended there. This worked out well until the Christmas holidays.

The Saturday after Christmas, I went to the store. On the way back, I say my man friend. I stopped to talk with him. We slipped into the back of the shop and got in his car for a little smooching. He gave me a gift as I was getting ready to go home. Then he jokingly asked where his gift was. I responded that all I had was me. He said, "I'll take you!" We kissed some more and he asked if I really meant what I had said. I answered "yes" but he would have to wait a little longer. I really was ready, but I had to get back home. We talked and smooched until we knew that there was no turning back. We went to his sister's house. He knew that she would not be at home. We had waited seven months for the right moment and we thought that this was it. However, he was a big disappointment – it didn't go well at all. We sat around and talked for a while before I realized how late it had gotten. It was around 10 pm before I got back home. That was really bad news!

He took me home and before I reached my door, I could tell that there was a party going on. I knocked lightly (really afraid to knock at all) and got no answer. I went back out to the service station. I knew that my friend would be there waiting for me to call him. I told him that my mother would not answer the door. He suggested that I call her. When I did, she asked where I had been. I told her with a friend. She said that since I couldn't come home at the proper time, perhaps I should go back where I had been. I was scared half to death but too proud to tell her that was not what I wanted to do. I hung up the phone.

When I told my friend what she has said, he was very obviously upset – sorry for getting me in trouble. I later found out that he was really afraid for himself. He took me to another sister's house. They were having a party. His sister was nice to me, but it was obvious that she was upset with him. She took him into another room and although I couldn't understand what was being said, I knew that she was not a happy camper. When they came back into the room, he mingled for a little while. She asked me if I wanted something to eat or drink. I was too upset to eat but said that I would take something to drink. I really felt like a fool when she came back with a glass of milk and explained that she did not have any more sodas. She didn't have to say it, but I got the message loud and clear – "you're just a little girl."

My friend introduced me to another sister. Shortly afterwards, we went back to the house where we had been earlier. This was the house of one of the sisters that I met at the party. When she came in later, I heard her tell him that she would allow me to stay the night, but I would have to be out of there early the next morning because "she was not going to get caught up in no mess." We slept on the sofa but I don't think that either of us rested.

The next morning, his sister's kitchen was filled with other family members. They fixed breakfast. Before we had finished eating, the heat was on. There was an onslaught of questions, mostly directed at him. They were angry with him because they were "forced to lie for him." One sister kept asking what they were supposed to tell Sophia (an alias). Finally, I asked who they were talking about. He had no choice but to tell me when his sister said, "If you don't tell her, I will." He told me that Sophia was his wife. His sister told me that he had a child. I was so stunned that I was speechless. Then I was so angry that I found tears rolling down my face. His sister tried to console me but there was nothing that she could say to do so. When I finally found words, I thanked his sister for allowing me to stay the night. I told him to call me a cab so that I could go home. Before the call could be made, a call came in. When it was over, his sister said to him, "I have not seen you since last night. I don't know where you are and don't know who you were with last night. The cops are looking for you. Now, take your little girl home and I suggest that you go home." They apologized for him getting involved with me. It was just as he had said the night before – they spoiled him rotten but acted like they were his mother. As I was leaving one of them asked how I could see anything exciting about a man who was **twice my age.** I was stunned, again, as I found out that he was thirty-two, not twenty-three.

Of course, when I got home, it was not a happy scene. My mother had gone into her quiet mode. She was furious when she was quiet. One had to walk easy when she was quiet. She sent me to my room and said that she would talk to me later. Now, I was really afraid. I took a bath and just waited. When we finally had that conversation, I didn't have much to say. I only answered questions and my answers were not what she wanted to hear. She told me that she was pressing charges against him (carnal knowledge). I became defiant, but careful. I told her that it was her fault that I had spent the night with him because she refused let me in and told me to go back where I had been. She said that I never had permission to go anywhere but to the store. True, but if she wouldn't let me in when I did come home, I had no place to go but back to him. She told me everything that she had found out about him – his wife and child, as well as his age. Therefore, since I was a minor, she could have him charged. I told her that nothing had happened. As far as I was concerned, nothing did. He couldn't make it happen. I don't know how she found out that I was seeing this man. Only two of my girlfriends knew and she didn't know them. She dug around enough to find out about him, but didn't know what was happening in her own home. That was hard for me to believe.

The next day, my mother took me downtown to file charges against my man friend. I answered each question with a minimal response. My story was this: I didn't know that he was thirty-two. I didn't know that he was married. We never had sex. My mother didn't answer the door when I came home. He took me home with him. I didn't know the address. We were alone until late that night when other people came in. I didn't know them. I came home alone in a cab. The end result was that the charges could not be filed. No witnesses, plus my account of what happened equaled no crime that would hold up in court. There was also a hint that my mother could be questioned regarding her actions (not letting me in when I did come home), which could possibly be viewed as reckless endangerment. Good for me – I won, she lost!

Happy New Year!

It was the beginning of 1960. Well, I guess you can only imagine that it was not a happy New Year for me. I was grounded indefinitely. I went to school and church. I was told to stay away from the service station. However, I was bad enough to call my ex-man friend to tell him that I wanted to talk with him. One morning, he met me at a street car stop and took me to school. I got my revenge by telling him that I understood why we couldn't get it on. He wasn't just anxious – he was too old to "cut the mustard." I knew that it was a low blow but I think that what hurt him the most was that I told him that if he had told me the truth, I still would have allowed him to do what we wanted because I was not a virgin and he was dumb if he thought that I was. Seven months of waiting for the right time with my man friend had gotten me nothing but back in the dog house and the dog was the only one who benefited. To make matters worse, I had learned how to control my urges, yet I was still subject to the urges of the dog. At least, I was back to wanting to claw his eyes out and to find a way to get revenge against him. I spiraled lower and lower into what seemed like a bottomless pit. I think that I began to hate myself as much as I hated my mother. Sometimes, I felt like I would be better off if I were dead. However, I learned to hide behind the mask of a happy face. I learned how to go through the motions.

Around the middle of January, I found myself in more hot water. My mother informed me that the police had come to our house and that I had been accused of breaking the window on the streetcar and assaulting a man. That accusation was only half true. I did break the window on the streetcar, but I did not assault the man. That event occurred on the same afternoon that my mother claimed that she saw me somewhere that I should not have been -- the day before Thanksgiving. As I mentioned earlier, there had been a fight in the tunnel at DuPont Circle. When the fight was over, we got on the streetcar. It was later than usual and there were quite a few of us. Some of us had to stand up.

At some point, an elderly man got on the streetcar and was pushing his way to the back, fussing because he could not find a seat. I was sitting down and offered him my seat. When I got up to allow him to sit down, he started swearing at us, calling us heathens who had no respect. Now you know that I was fuming. I'd just given this man my seat and instead of saying "thank you", he starts mouthing at us.

Now, you have to consider the times in order to understand what really ticked me off. The white folks were still having a difficult time understanding that we had the same rights as they did. Black folks did understand that we didn't have to keep putting up with their insults. We would insult them back. Well, I worked myself into a tizzy trying to think of something inappropriate to say to this old man. I arrived at my stop before I had the opportunity to enter into a verbal conflict with him. When I got off of the streetcar, I swung my gym bag against the window in an effort to get his attention. I had forgotten that my shoes were in the bag. The window broke and I was out of there in a flash. I ran a marathon!! I was home in less than five minutes, even after ducking through alleys so no one could follow me. It would normally take ten to fifteen minutes from that streetcar stop to my house. I honestly had no intentions of doing anything other than to get the man's attention so that I could say something ugly to him. My friends came by my house and told me that the man had been cut by broken glass and was taken to the hospital. That was all a lie meant to scare me. I must admit – I was scared.

Two months went by and nothing was heard about the incident. Then in January, when I thought that it was over, the police came. The irony of the whole thing was they would have never known it was me if a girl from another school had not "fingered me." I was becoming very friendly with her brother and she didn't like me. Therefore, when the police went to the all-black school in Georgetown, she became an informer. When I explained how the incident happened, the detective believed me. The man was not hurt but my mother had to pay for the window, which was taken from my babysitting money.

Sweet Sixteen

I would try to stay out of trouble, but it wouldn't last long. I always managed to get into something. One day I could be this wonderful loving child. The next, I could be a vengeful, bitter imp. I was bittersweet. I got along well with most people but I hated myself and my mother.

It goes without saying that I hated the dog. I spent a lot of time trying to figure out how to kill him. It seemed that everything that I could think of turned out to be a bad idea. I thought that I was smart, but I wasn't smart enough to get out of his grasp. One idea that I came up with to get back at him should have resulted in my escape. It didn't. He was a bootlegger. He would buy liquor and sell it after hours for a much higher price than it would cost at the store. If I was at home alone at night and a "customer" came to make a purchase, I was allowed to make the transaction. I remember that just before my sixteenth birthday, a man came to make a purchase. I recognized him as a private detective that worked in one of the stores in which we shopped. I was a little nervous because he kept trying to convince me to sell him the liquor in spite of my insisting that I didn't know what he was talking about. He called names of a couple of people that I knew but I still refused to sell him anything. About two hours later, one of the persons that he had named came to make a purchase and I refused to sell him anything. I knew that it was a trap. That would have been an excellent opportunity to get the dog in trouble, but I was afraid that I would be arrested too. That's when I came up with the idea to set another trap.

I had not been babysitting much because my main "client" had moved. I decided that I would start taking money from the liquor funds. I would buy things that I knew would get my mother's attention. I waited until I knew that we would all be home at the same time. At dinner time, I came to the table wearing a nice choker. My mother asked where I got it and I told her that I'd bought it. When she asked where I got the money, I nervously told her that I had found it. She fell right into my plan and kept questioning me. I finally "admitted" that the dog had given it to me. The next question was why I would lie if he gave me the money. My response was that he had told me not to tell her that he was giving me money. She turned the questioning on him but it didn't work in my favor. He told her that she had to know that I was lying because I was always lying about something. I refused to change my story. I could tell that she didn't know who to believe. However, I knew that I had given her something to think about. It really didn't turn out as I expected. He let me know that he knew that I was stealing his money. I let him know that there was nothing he could do about it – either I would continue to take what I wanted from the funds or I would not sell anymore liquor. He started clearing out most of the money every day. So, I told my mother about the private detective that was trying to buy liquor. She told me not to sell to anyone anymore. My mother released my punishment shortly after that. I don't know if it was coincidence or because I had just turned sixteen.

I was doing well in school and thought that I wanted to be a nurse. That idea was squashed when I went out one day and saw a trail of blood on our block. A lot of it was thick and looked sickening. It absolutely turned my stomach. Nevertheless, I had not outgrown the need to know. Therefore, I followed the trail to the service station. I then backtracked and followed it past my house and onward for another block. Somebody had lost a lot of blood? Later, the news spread that one of the neighbors that lived on the block of the black homeowners had been stabbed. He had walked those two and a half blocks in an effort to get help. He did survive. Nonetheless, every time that I saw those stains (water wouldn't wash them away for a long time), I would imagine trying to deal with someone seriously hurt and knew that I wouldn't be able to handle being a nurse.

My mother urged me to pursue a career in cosmetology. I simply could not get her to understand that, although I could work wonders in making my hair look good, I could not do other people's hair. However, upon her insistence, I did apply at the Martha Washington School of Cosmetology and was accepted. Unfortunately, I did not get the experience. I dropped out of school after graduating from the ninth grade.

I was so messed up I couldn't do right even when I tried. **But God** was starting to get my attention. I started going to a Pentecostal church which my mother was attending. I only went because I liked the music. However, every now and then, some small seed of the Word would begin to take root. I wish that I could say that I got saved at that point, but I can't. I was headed to hell in the fast lane by way of the church.

BUT GOD! I was sinking further and further into pit. Yet, He held fast to me. He loved me when I couldn't love myself. Once again, my mind thinks on Jeremiah 29:11 - For I know the thoughts that I think toward you, says the Lord, thoughts of peace and not of evil, to give you a future and a hope.

Not everyone who says to me, "Lord, Lord," will enter the
kingdom of heaven, but only he who does the will of my
father who is in heaven.

~ Matthew 7:21 ~
(NIV)

Chapter Eleven:
Church Folks

From this point, most of my story revolves around the church. I want to briefly backtrack to cover the beginning of my church experiences. My first recollection of church begins with my memories of living with my grandmother. My sisters and I went to Sunday school and I was almost always interested in the stories from the Bible. I was approximately six years old when I got baptized. I was the exception to the rule. The rule was that children had to be at least twelve years old before they were allowed to get baptized. I kept begging my grandmother to let me get baptized. What I really wanted was to be able to eat the crackers and drink the "wine" that they had at the church during the communion service. One Sunday, the preacher told my grandmother that he would baptize me because I kept insisting that I *needed* to be baptized. I was included in the next baptism. I was actually baptized in a river. We marched from the church to the river. When the last person was dipped, we would march back to the church for communion. After baptism, I could drink from the little glass and eat the little piece of cracker. I would always be so excited when it was the Sunday for communion.

I don't remember much about church during the short period between coming to DC and going to New York to live with my aunt. While in New York, my cousin and I would go to church almost every Sunday. Sometimes, my uncle would go with us, but my aunt never went. The church was large and looked like a cathedral - nothing like the little wooden church in North Carolina.

When I came back to DC to live with my mother, I became more aware of church activities. My mother kept us in church from early morning to late afternoon on Sundays and quite often during the week. That church was really different. It was in a house. I later learned that this type of church was considered to be a "store front" church. We had to participate in almost everything, i.e., Sunday school (I was teaching the little kids when I was ten years old), the Junior Choir, Junior Ushers, as well as Christmas and Easter programs. We had to walk approximately twelve blocks to church. It seemed as though the only places we went were to school and to church. The adults in our church were very staunch and strict. All the ladies wore their "Sunday best" and the few men always wore suits, no matter how hot it would get. The children were so "dressed up" that we couldn't play, for fear of getting dirty. There were so many "don'ts" that we were often afraid to do anything. It was almost like everything was a sin. We couldn't play card games, such as Old Maids or Go Fish. It was wrong for the children to say that someone was telling a lie. We couldn't go to sleep in church after we had reached a certain age. Adults were discouraged from wearing red because red represented Jezebel and of course, drinking and smoking were definitely a NO, NO. The pastor and his wife were like a couple of prunes. It was at that church that I first began to distrust church folks.

As children, we were expected to be little angels. However, many of the adults would say one thing and do another. They had a different set of rules. The thing that really set me to thinking negative about church folks was the pastor of our church. As I said, we were expected to be little angels, but they would do what we were taught (by them) was wrong.

During the first two years of living with my mother, I went to the pastor's house after school. His wife would care for me until one of my sisters would come to take me home. They were raising their grandson and a niece. One day, the niece and I were playing outside and she told me that she wanted to teach me a new game. I was eight or nine and she was, maybe, twelve. She began to fondle me and I made her stop. When I asked what kind of game she called that, she said that her uncle (the pastor) "played" the game with her. I was already familiar with that game (remembering my uncle) and wanted no part of it. I was surprised that a pastor would do this sort of thing. It was wrong! She must have known that it was wrong because she begged me not to tell anyone. She said that she would get in trouble if her uncle found out that she had told someone. That night, I told my mother that I was big enough to come home by myself and wait for my sisters to come home. She agreed to let me try it to see if it would work out.

As I grew older, I noticed more and more that church folks weren't what they claimed to be. As some of them would say about the others, he or she was wearing two hats on one head. That was my observation until I reached the age of thirteen or fourteen. Then I became one of them. I would act one way around certain people and another way when out of their presence.

Shortly, after moving to the Adams-Morgan apartment, we stopped going to that church. I asked for and received permission to go to church with one of my friends. Her mother would take us and pick us up after the service. After we were dropped off, we would go in the front door, get a program and leave by way of the side door. We would take our offering money and go to the neighborhood carry-out to play the pin ball machine until it was almost time for service to end. Then, we would go back to the church and wait for my friend's mother to pick us up. This was our routine except when her grandmother would go with us or when the Men's Chorus would sing. The Men's Chorus sang really well and we would stay on the Sundays that they sang.

I don't remember when my mother started attending the Pentecostal church, but I think that I must have been about thirteen years old. I first went with her to the church for a New Year's Eve service. After the New Year, I started going with my mother to the Pentecostal church. I really did like going to that church because of the music. The church was established by the founder of a very popular quartet group in DC. This was the church where I joined the "church folk" that wore two hats on one head. The "two hat" folks were hypocrites.

Now, I need to make a disclaimer. I am in no way saying that all the people in the church are phony. Even in this time in which we live, the church has and will always have folk who will come for whatever reason and never make a real commitment to follow after Christ. However, that should not deter us if we have made a commitment. When we say, "Whosoever will, let him come", we must understand that there will be wheat and there will be tares. When I speak of "church folk," I am usually referring to tares - the weeds that can cause problems with the growth and harvest of the wheat.

Spectator

The thing that most drew me to the Pentecostal church was the music and the dancing. There was so much excitement in the air! I would watch in amusement as people - young and old - seemed to lose control of themselves. Some would dance, others would run, and some would get so excited that they would lose their ability to speak clearly. This activity would be the highlight of my week. Week after week, I would watch. I observed so well that I knew when to expect certain people to do "their thing."

The pastor of this church was a very kind lady. She would encourage all of us to learn more about the Jesus that we talked and sang about. When she got up to preach, she would have the church secretary read the passage of Scripture that she would be using for the sermon. This lady was not the recipient of a seminary degree. In fact, she did not have much traditional education. However she did know what the Bible said. If someone would read something different than what she asked for, she had a way of letting the reader read the incorrect passage and then she would repeat what she wanted until the correct passage was read. Whenever this occurred, we would get a mini sermon (before the main sermon) about the importance of knowing the Bible. She may not have been a scholar, but she preached what she knew. Over the years, I came to believe that she was one of the few people, in the church, who live what she preached. I loved and respected her, at times, more that my own mother. Some seven years later, I became her "right arm."

The church secretary was a seventeen year old who was obviously the favorite of the pastor and some of the members of the church. That girl would dance almost non-stop. Our church was a very small store front. In the front section of the church was a large metal pole (about 4 inches square) that ran from the floor to the ceiling. The choir sat in the immediate area near that pole. Well, the secretary was also a choir member and she would dance all over that section. Sometimes, she would come so close to that pole that I would get nervous. I wondered how she could dance so (with her eyes closed) and never touch that pole. It was absolutely amazing! One Sunday, she did hit the pole. Her head hit that pole so hard that it sounded like a loud gong. The people were staring wide-eyed, the musician stopped playing, but she kept dancing. I was convinced that she was really for real or plain crazy.

The chairman of the Deacons (at the time that I joined the church) was another source of amazement for me. Our church had small wooden folding chairs. That deacon would start testifying (sounded like preaching) and sometimes he would get so happy (anointed?) that he would start walking up and down the aisle. Occasionally, he would literally walk the chairs. By that, I mean that he would step over the top edges of the chairs and walk all the way to the back of the church. Granted, that would only be about ten rows, but none of those chairs would fall while he was walking them. Amazing!! A small child could knock one of those chairs over but this man (who was no light weight) walked over the tops of them without causing them to fold or fall!

The head missionary was another lady that made a favorable impression on me. She had the ability to teach the Scriptures so that even a child, such as me, could understand. She was stern in her teaching, but there was a kindness about her that kept you listening and wanting to hear more.

Imitator

I've mentioned a few of the people for which I had much respect. I continued to watch and observe their actions, in and out of service. As I watched, I learned how to imitate them. On Sunday afternoons, my friends could hardly wait for me to come home. I had my very own "Side Show", mimicking those crazy people with their dancing, running, shouting and jumping. I did not make fun of the people that I mentioned above, except for the church secretary. There was no way that I was going to miss telling my friends about the big gong! There were others that I admired and there were others who, as the time went by, I discovered were wearing many hats. Many of them had a direct impact on my life. I will tell you about some of them later, as I continue my story.

I joined that church about a year after I became the victim of the dog. In time, I began to learn quotes from the Bible. One of them was that the devil comes to steal, kill, and destroy. Indeed, he did "kill" me. In spite of going to church and enjoying the services, I remained someone that I didn't like. Because I didn't like myself, I was convinced that nobody else liked me. Therefore, after joining the church, I became someone else. I didn't only join church; I joined the "church folk." As in the previous church, it seemed as though everything was a sin. The girls could not wear pants or make up, no cut out shoes or short dresses, your arms had to be covered at least to the elbow, and going to dances and movies was absolutely a bad influence. Nonetheless, I was really a great pretender. I played my part well. I was rebellious, defiant, and low self-esteem was my middle name. I was all of those things, but I hid behind the pretense of being a nice little church girl. In reality, I was still sinking.

BUT GOD! In the words of a song writer, "He looked beyond my faults and saw my need." He knew that I needed someone who loved me in spite of me. Tenderly, He beckoned me – Come. As He gently prodded me with a song, a Word, or a seed being planted by the pastor, I slowly, very slowly, began to pay attention.

Marriage is miserable unless you find the right person that is your soul mate.

Marvin Gaye

CHAPTER TWELVE:
I Was A Teenage Bride

S hortly after I joined the Pentecostal church, I became friends with the daughter of the choir directress. I need to tell you a little about this family – more church folk - because it had a major impact on my life. The choir directress's husband was a deacon in the church. Shortly after the church was organized, the pastor disbanded the quartet group that she had founded. The choir directress and her husband reorganized the group and changed the name. They had top billing in the city along with several other well-known singing groups. The couple also had a son who would come to church every now and then. It was obvious that he did not want to be there. Their daughter, their niece, and I became close friends.

On Christmas, I was invited to my friends' home for dinner. I was absolutely shocked at some of the things that I observed. This was the home of leaders in the church and I saw some things that blew my mind. For starters, wine (real wine) was served with dinner. After dinner, the adults went to the upper level of the house and the teenagers went down to the basement to play music and dance. My friend went back to the dining room and got some vodka that had been hidden in a Christmas figurine. The vodka belonged to her mother. I found out that her mother always had a bottle in the house. We all had some "spiked punch." Evidently, my friend's grandmother had been drinking something as well. While we were in the basement, the grandmother suddenly appeared at the door. She came half way down the stairs and did a very sexually suggestive belly roll. My friends thought that it was funny. I was stunned that the "church mother" would even think of doing something like that, especially in front of the children.

Later, we decided to go to the movies. By the time we got there, I was feeling the dinner wine and the one drink of "punch." Therefore, we didn't get to see the entire movie because I kept talking and giggling. After a couple of warnings, we were put out of the theater. When we returned to my friend's house, she and her boyfriend disappeared for a while. Her brother tried to take advantage of me and probably would have succeeded if I hadn't been afraid that we would get caught. By the time that I left to go home, I had seen a lot that should not have taken place in a "Christian" home.

I tell you about this family because I later married the son. What a devastating mistake. That was a marriage created in hell. I should not have expected anything different. After all, I was the one who was going to tear Satan off of his throne and claim it as my own. Instead, I was swept into the tangled web of his evilness.

The summer after I graduated from ninth grade was both good and bad. It was good because my mother did not punish me at the drop of a hat and I wasn't confined to the house as much. It was also good because my grandmother came from North Carolina to stay with us. Therefore, the dog couldn't get access to me as often. Mama and I shared my bedroom and she was home most of the time.

My friend's mother helped me to get a summer job, working on a construction site. Her husband was a brick layer and foreman on a project where a large apartment complex was being built. My sister and one of her friends also got a job with us. As the buildings were completed, our job was to make sure that the units were ready for rental. We gave the units a thorough "cleaning", i.e., making sure that no tar remained on the wooden tile floors, no paint on the bathroom tile or fixtures, and no stains on the white walls, stove tops or cabinets. It was hard work and most of the time, the apartments were hot and there were no fans available.

The summer break turned out to be bad because I quit the job and didn't have as much money as I'd planned for the beginning of the next school year. I had put clothes in lay-a-way and I would also need money for school uniforms and supplies. I quit the job because one of the foremen would deliberately say and do things to make us angry. We had been on the job for approximately a month. The foreman would talk to us as if we were a piece of garbage.

When we started working on the project, there were about ten women working. Every week, the afternoon foreman would fire one or two of us until there were only the four of us – my friend's mother, and the three of us that were hired because of our association with her and her husband. When we arrived for work in the mornings, the morning foreman would give us our assignments. In the early afternoon, the other foreman would come in fussing and cussing. He would have us stop what we were doing and start something else. He would always use a negative tone and nasty words.

One day, he was angry because the four of us were not getting enough apartments ready for rental (after he had fired six people). He made some racist remarks and threatened to fire us if we hadn't finished a certain amount of units before the end of the day. We knew that there was no way that we would finish, but we didn't say anything. Later, he came back and started yelling at us because we were not moving fast enough. Again, he used a racist remark as he was leaving. I had had enough. I told the girl that I was working with that I was quitting. She said that she was too. I started getting my things together and told her that I would meet her at the car. She said that she was going to finish out the week and then quit. I left her to finish what we had started. She was fired the next day.

Another reason that the summer wasn't good was because, in spite of going to church and trying to do better, I went from bad to worst. I went to most of the quartet singing programs – almost every Sunday night. The more I went, the more I learned about church folk. Married men were chasing women who were not their wives. Folk "singing heaven down," dancing, and "praising" and as soon as the service was over, many of them were off to sleeping around. Many of the women being chased were willing "victims," some of them doing the chasing instead of being chased.

Summer had barely started when I got involved with another man-friend. This time it was different. I knew that he was married and had a child. I don't remember the details of how the relationship got started; I only know that I allowed it to happen because I didn't want another boy-friend. We would manage to see each other almost every week. I got pregnant in less than two months after the beginning of the relationship. I liked this man and believed that he really cared about me. He immediately knew when I got pregnant. He actually cried when he said, "I just got you pregnant." I didn't believe him. How could he know? However, he insisted that he did know. He was right. When I told him that I was late, he said that he wanted me to go away with him and we could always be together. At that moment, it was over for us. He had said the wrong thing. Without hesitation, I heard myself telling him that it would never happen. I told him that if he would leave his wife for me, it would only be a matter of time before he would leave me for someone else. I immediately broke up with him without giving it a second thought. From that day, I refused to call him or take any calls from him.

I was afraid to tell my mother that I was pregnant, so I went to my oldest sister to talk with her, hoping that she could help me. She did try, but to no avail. She and my mother got into an argument and I wouldn't go back home. After a week, my mother agreed to let me stay with my sister.

In the meanwhile, my friend's brother was constantly trying to get with me. I finally told him that I was pregnant and couldn't get involved with him. When he asked who the father was, I lied and told him that the father was dead. He insisted that he didn't care that I was pregnant and that he would marry me if I would change my mind. It sounded tempting, but something kept telling me not to do it. I should have followed my mind. I still worried about what my mother was going to do. My sister really could not afford to take care of me and a baby. She was pregnant with her fourth child and they were barely making ends meet. In spite of me not really liking the boy, I agreed to go out with him. We dated for almost a month and I decided that marriage might be the best thing for me to do.

When I told his sister that we were thinking about getting married, she suggested that we have a double wedding. She had been dating one of my friends and he was in the army. We got a little excited about the idea and she talked her mother into allowing her to get married. We started making plans for the wedding, not having a clue of what we were doing. Her mother took over the plans and we just went along with what she said.

My mother went along with the idea, assuming that I was marrying the father of my baby. When I told her that my future husband was not the father, she went into a tongue lashing that made me decide that when I did get married, it wouldn't be soon enough. She was not concerned about me. She was concerned about her being embarrassed if his family found out that their son was not the father. She appeared to be shocked when I told her that he knew that he was not the father. I suggested that if he wanted to take on the responsibility of a father, she should be glad for me. NOT! She kept going on about what people would think and made it clear that I was not good enough to marry into that family. She said that I would cause problems for everybody. Little did she know that this family that she held in such high esteem were nowhere near what she believed. Oh, the thoughts that ran through my mind. I wanted to tell her off, but I knew better. Even when I was angry, I knew not to show any disrespect towards her.

A couple of weeks before the wedding, I told his mother that I was pregnant and that the baby was not his. She didn't say much. She said that if he was willing to father the child, it would be up to him and nothing would be different as far as she was concerned. I had made up my mind that I would be the perfect little wife. A week before the wedding, I moved my few belongings into their home. His mother was busy making all of the arrangements. My mother agreed to help with the finances. She said very little to me during that week and that was fine with me.

The only one of us who was able to marry without parental consent was my friend's fiancé. A week before the wedding, we went to apply for our marriage licenses. I was able to get mine but she could not get hers. Even with her parent's approval, she was too young. She and her fiancé had to go to Virginia to get a license. They were able to get it, but not in time for the wedding.

One day before the wedding, things began to go very wrong. It should have been a warning to call off the wedding, but back in the day, pregnant and not married was a total disgrace. There were so many things that went wrong, I couldn't believe it. My sister-in-law to be did not receive her license on that Saturday, as she thought she would. My pastor discovered, on Saturday, that her license to perform the marriage ceremony had expired. She had to call another minister to perform the ceremony. That was a disappointment. I found out, at the rehearsal, that my mother-in-law to be had chosen the daughter of my baby's father to be one of the flower girls – my flower girl. Sheer coincidence. Nonetheless, it was quite disturbing for me – wondering if it was indeed a coincident.

My wedding day was one miserable day for me. I did not wear white. That was a "tell-tell" sign that I was not a virgin. I just could not make myself wear white and although

I tried not to show it, I was embarrassed, knowing what the spectators were probably whispering. My friend should not have worn white either. I knew that she was not a virgin, but she insisted that she was.

Added to my misery was the fact that my baby's father was at the wedding. As we were waiting outside the church, he looked directly at me as if he was about to cry. As I approached the door, he cut in front of me and whispered, "You're having my baby." I was terrified, thinking that someone might have heard him.

When the ceremony was over, things got worse. My mother-in-law had asked one of our friends to drive us to the reception. After we had gotten into the car, the driver's girlfriend came up, with a friend, insisting that they ride with us. An argument about who was going to ride in the car ended with my husband sitting up front and me sitting in the back with the two girls. Picture how dumb that looked. What a mess! If there was no happiness then, I knew that there would be none later. I had often heard the expression, "The way you start a marriage is the way it will end." What an indictment. For me, it proved to be absolutely true.

The following week, the minister who performed our wedding ceremony, came to bring us our marriage certificates. It showed the date of marriage as being October 5th. It should have been October 2nd. When I pointed this out, the minister said that he had to change the date because he did not have my sister-in-law's license when we got married. I made a fuss about the lie, forgetting that the whole issue surrounding my marriage was built on lies that I had told, especially about the paternity of my baby. The marriage was bound for destruction, no matter how much I intended to be a good wife.

Sixteen years old, pregnant, married, and miserable. My life was a total mess. I didn't have a clue about the hell that I had just stepped into. **But God!** God had a plan for my life and He was not about to allow Satan **or me to** abort it.

What the devil meant for evil was going to be used to push me into my destiny. The negative issues, that I had to deal with, took an opposite effect than previous negative issues. Instead of becoming more bitter, I began to tone down. I began to pay attention to more than the music. I listened to the Word. Again, I wish that I could say that I got saved. I can't. However, I can say that I wanted to know more about salvation. As I paid more attention to the Word, I began to think that I could never be saved. I had done so much wrong that I actually believed that I was already condemned to hell. Therefore, I kept wearing the hats that church folk wore.

But God!! I kept hearing one particular Word that stayed with me. "You shall know the truth and the truth shall make you free." John 8:32 (NKJV)

Choose your life's mate carefully. From this one decision will come 90 percent of all your happiness or misery.

H. Jackson Brown, Jr.
(Author)

CHAPTER THIRTEEN:

Miserable Wife –

Happy Mother

O n our wedding night, my husband and I got so drunk that neither of us could remember what we did. After the reception, we had an "after party." The church guests had left and, for the most part, the only guest remaining were the teenagers and young adults. At some point, I decided to go to bed and left everyone else to finish the celebration. The next thing that I recall was hearing glass breaking. I woke up to find my husband "trapped" in the corner of our bedroom. He was so drunk that he didn't have sense enough to turn around. So, he was stuck between the bed and the dresser. There he was - two steps forward into the wall and a few steps backwards into nothing. It was a miracle that he didn't cut his feet on the glass that he had dropped. I watched him for a few minutes and then went back to sleep. I don't know how he got out of that corner or when he finally came to bed.

For a couple of weeks, things were okay. I did what housewives do. While he was at work, my sister-in-law and I cleaned the house, did laundry, and cooked. About two weeks after the wedding, I became the victim of physical abuse. This first incident, although minor, was both embarrassing and enraging. We were at one of the Sunday night quartet programs. By this time, I knew that my husband had no interest in church. As usual, some of us had gone out for a smoke. We went to the parking lot and I got into the car. The others were standing around talking and laughing. Seemingly, from out of nowhere, my husband appeared and reached through the window and slapped me in my face. I was stunned. "What in the world was wrong with him?" I thought. He began to accuse me of being outside with one of the singers. There were about four men and three women standing around the car. He thought that he had heard someone flirting with me. Actually, I was not talking with anyone. When the others convinced him that nothing was happening, he didn't even apologize for hitting me.

When the others went back into the building, he told me to stay in the car with him. I didn't know whether to stay or not. I wondered, "Would he hit me again when everyone else was gone?" Although the question ran through my mind, in order to keep from creating another scene, I stayed. I was somewhat afraid but he didn't know it. After everyone had gone back inside, I lit into him verbally. I boldly informed him that if I were not afraid of hurting the baby, there definitely would have been a fight when he hit me. We talked and I told him that if my mother hadn't raised me, he certainly couldn't do it and that I had no intentions of becoming his punching bag. His response was to inform me that I couldn't beat him. Since he weighed approximately a hundred and seventy pounds and I only weighed approximate ninety eight pounds, I knew that I could not beat him. Nonetheless, I let him know that I would die trying to defend myself and that if I could get in just one good punch, nothing else would matter.

The remainder of the night was an uneasy silence between us. When he wanted to be intimate, I informed him that I would not be a woman who he could beat up on and then allow him to act as if nothing had happened. This first incident ended with us not talking to each other for a couple of days. I would get up in the morning to prepare his lunch. I had dinner ready when he got home, but I said no more to him than was necessary. I'd never been one to hold a grudge (except against the dog) so the silent treatment only lasted a few days.

The next incident happened when I had gone for my doctor's appointment. This time, it was verbal abuse. It snowed really hard that day. In inclement weather, the streetcars would often shut down. On that day, I had gotten half way home when the streetcar could go no further. The snow had fallen quickly and heavily. I walked for about a half hour to forty five minutes to get to my aunt's house. When I called home, my husband was furious. He claimed that he had called the clinic and was told that I hadn't been there. I knew he was lying. We argued more when I told him that I was spending the night with my aunt. He didn't believe me and instructed me to take a cab home. I told him to come and get me. There was no way that I was going home without proof of where I was. Reluctantly, he agreed to come to get me. When we got home, he was still trying to argue. I refused to respond. I knew that he was angry, but he didn't hit me. He didn't work when the weather was bad (he was a construction worker). The next few days with him being at home were strained, to say the least.

It snowed a lot that year. It seemed as though it would snow every Thursday. On one of those snowy weekends, it began to snow just as we left the church. When we got home, I slipped and fell down the stairs. I was a little shaken up, but the pain was not enough to cause concern. My mother-in-law insisted that I go to the hospital. It took us about an hour to make a fifteen minute trip. When we reached the hospital, there were wall to wall people in the emergency room. It was almost another hour before I was registered to be seen.

There was a woman in the emergency room with her husband. She kept begging for a doctor to see him. It was obvious that he was really sick. The receptionist repeatedly told us that due to the weather, some of the doctors had not arrived. After several hours, the man slumped and fell to the floor. Suddenly, the emergency room was filled with nurses and doctors. If there were only two doctor's on duty at the time (as had been indicated by the receptionist), we asked where all the other doctors had come from. I was seen within half an hour after the man died. Fortunately, my fall had not harmed me or the baby. That incident made a lasting impression on me. They had actually allowed that man to sit there and die. I vowed that I would never be a patient at that hospital. To this day, the only time that I go to that particular hospital is to visit someone who is an inpatient.

It's a Boy!!!

Well, the big day arrived! No one told me what to expect other than a lot of pain. I was not in any pain and coupled with the fact that the baby was not due for another month, when I couldn't stop going to the bathroom, I didn't associate it with going into labor. It was not until my mother-in-law came home from church that I was made aware that my water had broken and I was in labor. As I prepared to go to the hospital, I was somewhat nervous and could not understand why I was not feeling any pain. I was admitted to the hospital but still had not had the baby by the next morning.

Around mid-morning, a decision was made to induce my labor. I was told that this was necessary because it had been almost twenty four hours since my water had broken. By the time those doctors got through with me, I wanted to fight! Unlike the way things are done now, induction of labor was done manually – not by injection of medication to initiate the labor. I don't remember how long the process took. I only remember that every time the pain would begin to subside, a doctor would come in and try to move the baby forward. One of the doctors was not nice at all. When I complained that he was really hurting me, he said that I should have thought about the pain before I got pregnant. It was not what he said; it was the nasty way in which he said it. If I could have moved at that point, I would have inflicted some pain on him!

Finally, the pain of all pain and then I am told, "It's a boy." I was a mother, but they wouldn't let me see him. They said that I had to wait until they checked to make sure that he was alright. Later, they told me that, due to my blood type

(RH negative), there was a possibility that he would be a "blue baby" and, if so, he would have to have a blood transfusion. I had never heard of a "blue baby" and they were not doing a good job of helping me to understand what they were telling me.

I was only sixteen years old and it was assumed that I was not married. Therefore, I was told to call my mother so that she could sign for the transfusion, if necessary. That added insult to injury. When I arrived at the hospital, the intake person had automatically stamped "illegitimate" on my registration papers, in spite of the fact that I had checked "married" for marital status. When I asked why she had done that, she told me that all babies born to unwed mothers were illegitimate. I informed her that I was married and she redid the paperwork. When the baby was born and, since the assumption was still that I was not married, I was instructed to have my mother sign for any treatment that might be necessary for my son. It was all that I could do to keep myself from screaming at someone. I angrily informed them that my mother had nothing to do with my baby. If I couldn't sign the consent forms, no one would. I was angry at the thought of having to call my mother. The doctor finally took the time to confirm that my admission file indicated that I was married. It turned out well. My baby did not have to have a transfusion. However, I was warned that any future babies would most likely need transfusions.

I had decided to nurse my baby. That didn't last more than a week. He kept getting sick (vomiting and diarrhea). I took him back to the hospital and was told that I could no longer nurse him. The doctor had examined me as well as the baby. Apparently I had a fever which, according to the doctor, indicated that I probably had an infection somewhere in my body and that was the reason that my baby was getting sick. Thankfully, he was okay after a couple of days.

I enjoyed being a mother. Taking care of babies was nothing new for me. I had been babysitting since I was approximately nine/ten years old. Now, I had my own baby to care for. The fact that I had gotten pregnant at such a young age and, even worse, by a married man, was a source of the lowest self-esteem that I had ever suffered.

But God!! I may have been ashamed of myself but, I was never ashamed of this precious little baby that I had. I was so proud of every accomplishment that he made – those fat fingers that would hold on to my fingers, the smiles and happy baby sounds, the first time he rolled over by himself. Watching him as he learned to pull up or crawl and walk (by the time he was nine months old), made me so proud to be his mother. Everything he did made my otherwise miserable life, worth living.

To everything there is a season and a time to every purpose under the heaven.

Ecclesiastes 3:1

CHAPTER FOURTEEN:
Mama Said There'd Be Days
Like This

A Time to Be Born and a Time to Die

Approximately six or seven weeks after my son was born, my grandmother died. That was a very traumatic event for me, especially since someone had made a mistake in getting the word out. I received a call advising me that my grandfather had died. I managed to digest that news fairly well. "Gramps" had been in a nursing home. He had also had an amputation, as well as other illnesses. Therefore, the news of his death was not exactly unexpected. Two hours later, my cousin called to say that my grandmother, not "Gramps" had died. This news took me to another level of grief. I remember going to the front door as I tried to digest this new information. It didn't go down very well. Apparently, I fainted and someone found me lying on the floor at the door. I managed to pull myself together enough to take care of my son.

The day of Mama's funeral was one of the saddest days of my life. She was the first parental figure that I'd known. Calling her Mama was really acknowledging her as my mother. She was the only mother that I knew for the first four or five years of my life. Now Mama would be just a wonderful memory.

The family had gathered at my mother's house before the funeral (By this time she was actually living in a house). We were almost an hour late because no one could find my uncle (Mama's youngest son). As it turned out, he was at home, refusing to answer his phone. He was overwhelmed by Mama's death. When someone went to get him, he had not gotten dressed and was hardly able to get it together. Although I didn't get to see him often, this was the uncle that was one of my heroes. He was the strong, tall, strapping giant of the family. He genuinely liked children and was fun to be with. Therefore, when I saw him breaking down at the funeral, it added more to my pain.

After the funeral service, we went back to my mother's house. My uncle was like a stranger and I felt so bad for him. My emotions were all over the place and must have gotten the best of me. Once again, I fainted. This time, I came to in the emergency room of the same hospital that I'd sworn I would never go to again. Upon realizing where I was, my first words were "Get me out of here!" My family was concerned because my son was barely six weeks old and they wanted to be sure that nothing else was wrong. I assured them that they had two choices – take me home or I would get there the best way that I could. They took me home.

A Time to Love and a time to Hate

Several months after my baby was born, the abuse started again. I can't honestly say that I loved my husband, but I tried. He would start arguments over little or nothing. He was always careful to wait until we were home alone so that his family would not know that we were fighting. I was so miserable that I tried to leave, but I had no place to go. I was too proud to ask my mother if I could come back to stay with her. My sister really didn't have enough room. I called my aunt in New York and she didn't want to get involved. I was stuck.

My husband and I move to our first apartment when the baby was approximately four months old. The apartment was a very small unit in a rooming house. It was okay for me even though we had to share the bathroom with the tenant (a friend of the family) who lived on the same floor as we did. A few weeks later, my husband was drafted into the army. I was so happy! That joy was short-lived. He reported as required but returned home two days later. He said that he was rejected due to a minor medical problem. A week later, I told him that I was pregnant again. His reaction made me glad that he hadn't been gone long. He asked me if I was sure that the baby was his. As miserable as I was, I was faithful to him. I was hurt and angry. I told him that I had had enough of his mess and that I was going to leave him. He tried to pretend that he had only been joking. That may or may not have been true. I knew that if he had not been rejected by the Army, it definitely would not have been a joke. I did my usual after we argued – I shut down and gave him the silent treatment.

We had a regular cycle; a few days of peace followed by arguing over dumb stuff. During one of those arguments, he slapped me so hard that I developed a rash in the shape of his hand. Later that day, we visited his parents. His father asked what was wrong with my face. I told him that his son had slapped me. His father couldn't or wouldn't believe it. When he told my husband that he should be ashamed of himself, he actually denied hitting me. His uncle, who was severely abusive to his wife, said to him, "That's right, son, keep them in line. When they get out of place, beat the hell out of them." I had heard him make similar remarks on several occasions (usually after he had beaten his wife).

My husband did not go to church after we moved to our own apartment and he didn't want me to go. One Sunday, as I was leaving, he came out behind me and kicked me down the stairs. I had the baby in my arms and really hurt myself as I was trying to protect him from the fall. My husband stood at the door and watched as I picked myself up and left. When I got home from church, I told him if he ever hit me again, I would kill him in his sleep. He must have believed me because he didn't hit me again until a couple of years later.

We didn't argue as much after that incident. I don't know if it was because he believed that I would try to hurt him or if it was because I was pregnant. I will say that, during this phase of our marriage, it was the only time that he tried to act half-way decent. I craved a certain cut of steak and every payday, he would bring home enough steak to last the week. I worked on the weekends (child care) and stayed on the job from Friday to Sunday. Therefore, I had a little more peace. In early autumn, our friend found a larger apartment and we decided to move with her.

As the weather began to get cold, we discovered that our furnace required the use of coal. That would not have been so bad except that we were having issues regarding gaining access to the basement. We were constantly at odds with the landlord. Our living quarters was over a repair shop and the owners of the shop lived in back of it. They did not want us to access the basement or the back of the building (to empty trash) via the first floor hallway. They would lock the door so that we could not get into the hallway. I solved the access problem by throwing my trash out the window into the back yard and they would have to clean it up. Then I threatened to report the owner to Landlord and Tenants, regarding the furnace. When we finally obtained access to the basement, the furnace was not working properly. Sometimes we had heat and sometimes we didn't.

It was another hard winter and my husband was barely able to pay our share of the rent. Thankfully, my weekend job kept us with enough money for food. I also kept my friend's daughter during the week and she paid me for doing so. It wasn't very much because she kept my son on the weekends, but it was enough to help us make ends meet.

It's Another Boy!

Once again, I gave birth to a boy who was born before due date. He was due in April, but it was only February. He woke me up in the middle of an icy cold night. The pain was not severe but regular. I knew that I couldn't wait until daybreak to get to the hospital. We decided that it was too cold to take my son out so I went to the hospital alone in a taxi.

This time the labor was a little easier. I was in one of the best hospitals in the city and the care was much better than when I had my first son. I was placed on a monitor and for the most part, the nurse would tell me when I was having a contraction. A few hours after arriving at the hospital, my second son was born. Unlike my first delivery, I was able to hold my baby immediately. Most of his examination was done in the delivery room as they were taking care of me.

A Time to Weep and a Time to laugh

When I was taken to my room, my son was taken to the nursery. A few hours later, I was informed that my baby would need a transfusion. I was aware of the possibility that this would happen. I was told that he would be transferred to Children's Hospital. When my husband came to visit, he was informed of the situation and they provided transportation for him to take the baby to the hospital. Again, I was deprived of holding my baby. This time, it was for weeks! When I arrived home from the hospital, my husband and friend had already packed for us to move. It was too cold in the apartment for us to stay there. We moved back to my in-laws' house.

For almost a month, I was unable to see my son. I called the hospital daily and spoke with a nurse. I was always assured that he was doing fine. I couldn't go to see him. Back in the day, the rule was that after giving birth, you could not go out for six weeks unless there was an extreme emergency. This rule was strictly enforced by family and friends. However, when I was notified that my baby was being released from the hospital, I waited for no one. I went to get him! Oh happy day! Did I feel like dancing? You better know it!!!

It had been a difficult year - **But God!!** There were times that I absolutely wanted to kill my husband and had to tell myself that he wasn't worth me going to jail or hell. There were times when we could embrace each other and there were times when I didn't want to be anywhere near him. I did a lot of crying (secretly) but I learned to laugh more. I mourned the death of my grandmother but I wanted to dance when the "dog" died sometime during that year. Most importantly, I was learning, through all of the unpleasant situations, how to turn to God in prayer. Still not saved – **But God! He is merciful and gracious, slow to anger, and plenteous in mercy. He did not deal with me according to my sins** (See Psalm 103).

Let not the floodwater overflow me,
Nor let the deep swallow me up;
And let not the pit shut its mouth on me.

Psalm 69:15

CHAPTER FIFTEEN:
Like A Ship Without A Sail

The winter was very cold and my husband wasn't working much. His parents helped out with groceries by having us chip in to buy food for the entire household, except our friend. She had her own apartment on the third floor of the house and was doing well financially. Towards the end of March, my father-in-law pulled all of his men off of the project on which they were working. The weather was breaking but some days were very cold. The construction company, for which they were working, wanted them to continue working even if the temperatures were near freezing. To do so, would compromise the safety of the buildings. Approximately two weeks after my father-in-law refused to work the project, there was a windstorm and several of the apartment buildings collapsed. As a result, even when the weather broke, no one could go back to work, pending an investigation. They were off work for several months.

My First Miracle

At about the same time as we found out that the men in our family would be out of work indefinitely, we also were informed that my second son would need surgery. He had a hernia that needed to be removed. However, it could not be done until his blood count had reached a certain level. Meanwhile, we were instructed not to allow him to cry for more than a minute. The hernia would swell every time he cried and this put him in danger of rupturing his scrotum. It took about six to eight weeks to get his blood count up to the desired level. Unfortunately, before it reached that level, this precious little boy had sensed that he could get immediate attention when he cried. He was spoiled to the max!

In May or June, he was scheduled for the surgery. The Sunday before his scheduled date, I asked my pastor to pray for him. We believed strongly in anointing with oil. The pastor would not allow me to hold the baby while she anointed and prayed for him. Instead, she placed him on the lap of one of the mothers of the church. She told me that I could not hold him because I didn't have the "Holy Ghost" and could possibly be a hindrance to the prayer being answered. I would normally have resented not being able to hold my baby, but I decided that it was important to do what was best for him. Three days later, when I took him in for the surgery, the doctors could not find any sign of the hernia. They sent me home with the warning to check him regularly because "it could come back." To this day, it has not. Praise Jesus!

Shortly after our miracle, my husband decided to go back to North Carolina in order to seek employment. I stayed with my in-laws for a couple of months. Soon after my husband left, I had double trouble: One – I was pregnant again and two – somehow, my mother-in-law found out who was the father of my first son. She was getting money from him to "help take care of him." I had no clue until I received a phone call from my mother. I don't know what she was told, but she assumed that I was seeing him again. Therefore, this presented another opportunity for her to cut me down. When I questioned my mother-in-law, she stated that they needed all the help that they could get in order to keep food on the table and that "It was no more than right that my son's father should help." My husband had not sent any money and we seldom heard from him. I was really afraid of what might happen when he did return. My mother-in-law tried to assure me that he would not have to know. How could he not know?? Somebody had to tell my mother. That meant that other people were talking and eventually, my husband would also find out. To make matters worse, either my father-in-law or his brother took my son and introduced him to his father.

This happened on a weekend when I was at work. When I came home from work, my son had a new suit and a new pair of shoes. He said his "daddy" give them to him.

About mid-term of my third pregnancy, I moved in with my mother, along with my sister and cousin. For the life of me, I cannot remember how that move was initiated. I vaguely remember that my mother-in-law was complaining about having to take care of all the grandchildren (my two, as well as my sister-in-law's daughter). I suspect that my mother must have agreed to let me and my children live with her. God forbid that it should get out that she wasn't helping her own daughter.

I lived with my mother until my daughter was approximately three months old. It was also tight for her, financially. Her house was a rooming house and she was a nurse. My sister, my cousin, and another roomer paid their share of the rent. I had no income. Everyone, except the roomer who was not a family member, chipped in to buy food. However, the roomer kept us supplied with fresh rolls (baked daily) from his place of employment. He worked in the kitchen of an establishment and the employees were allowed to take any of the left-over food that they wanted. The only thing that I could contribute was the government rations that I received – powered milk, cheese, butter, peanut butter, and canned meat. My mother, being the excellent cook that she was, could take that stuff and place a tantalizing meal on the table. We were especially fond of the "sloppy Joe" that she would make from the canned meat and serve on a bun with coleslaw. There were no left-overs.

I don't think that my mother realized that my sister and my cousin were pregnant when they moved in. That presented a problem when all of the babies were born within a month of each other. I was the last one due, but the first to deliver. My baby was due in March. Due to my blood factor, the doctors induced labor in my seventh month. It's a girl!! Finally, a girl!! By the middle of February, we had a mini nursery in my mother's house.

They Took My Babies! ❀

For a while, we were all one big happy family. I provided day care for all of the children. My mother, sister, and cousin worked. With what my sister and cousin paid me for keeping their children, I was able to give my mother something to help out with household expenses. However, it was far too little to help much. I also made a little money by washing and ironing shirts for the roomer.

My husband was still "missing in action." Just as I was beginning to feel at ease, I was "knocked off my feet." When my daughter, was approximately three months old, my mother found out about the Welfare System. She told me to apply for financial assistance. She had been warned that the government would try to make her responsible for us. I was instructed to tell the social worker that my mother was not financially able to support me and my children and that I needed resources so that I could find an apartment for me and the children. As expected, I was given forms for my mother to provide proof of her income. Per instructions from my mother's "advisor," she refused to provide the information, stating that I was married and that she was not able to provide for us. The plan backfired! **They took my babies!** I was devastated – dumbfounded – a basket case! I went to them with all of my children and came back home with one. The social worker had told me that they needed to see my children before they would start the paperwork for my case. While I was filling out paper work, the social worker, told me that they would have to take my boys because, I could not have all of my children sleeping with me in one room. I was allowed to keep my daughter because "she was too young to be placed in the children's home." I could hardly believe my ears. In spite of being told why they were taking my boys, the rage was on. By the time I got back home, I was already back in the hate mode. My mother was to blame for them taking my babies. She appeared to be as shocked as I was. However, that was no consolation for me. I was without my babies. From that day, for a very long time, I could hardly function. I was in "auto-drive." The only thing that kept me half sane was my daughter, who was not taken from me. I cried for nights and days – devastated!

Shortly afterwards, my husband showed up. I imagined that his family had told him what happened with my sons. Strangely enough, that was not his major concern; there was a man in the house and I was ironing his shirts! Naturally, to my husband, that meant that I was involved with the man. I wasn't then, but for spite, I did get involved with the man, although there was no way for my husband to know. The affair didn't last long (just a few weeks) for two reasons. One – my cousin had her eyes on him after she broke up with her son's father. Two – the last thing that I wanted to do was get into a serious relationship. My cousin saw that we were becoming more than just friendly and she went after him with no reservations. Within a short period of time, they were a couple. It didn't bother me that he had discontinued the relationship with me. I knew that it would not work out. It did bother me that my cousin would betray me. We were living in the same house. How could she think that I hadn't noticed the sly remarks and sneaky looks between them? At night, she would slip into his room when she thought that I was asleep. One night, I decided to confront them. I needed them to know that I was not deaf, blind, or dumb. I went to her room and knocked on the door, knowing that she was not in there. Then I went to his room and walked in without knocking. They were speechless. I asked for something for a headache. She, obviously embarrassed, told me where to find it. I really did have a headache. I began suffering with migraine headaches less than a year after I got married. I said "good night" and closed the door. It infuriated me to think that my cousin, who until then, was actually like a sister, could actually think that I couldn't add two plus two and get four. I was so angry that my head began to pound. I was in so much pain – mentally and physically – that I began to sob. Later, when my sister came home from work, I heard them talking about the incident. She actually thought that I was crying about the man. Not hardly. If I had really wanted him, I could have played the same game that she was playing.

I decided not to say anything about it to either of them. The next day, I took his dirty shirts and placed them on her bed. I would speak to them, acting like nothing had happened.

During the few weeks that I was involved with the roomer, I also began drinking beer regularly. I thought that I needed something to help me sleep at night so that I wouldn't cry my heart out over the loss of my sons. My husband would come by about once a week but never offered anything to help out. All that he was interested in was if I was involved with the man in the house. Well, that finally exploded. He came by one Saturday morning, ranting and raving, claiming that he saw the man leave my room during the night. That was absolutely untrue! He wanted me to leave and go to where we used to live with his parents. He carried on so that my mother told him to "get out AND take his family with him." His family was me and my daughter. At that, my sister jumped in between us. She told me that I didn't have to leave if I didn't want. She told him that if he hit me, as he was threatening to do, she would whip his a--. She laid some verbal stuff on him that made him step back. My mother, in the meanwhile, was threatening to call the police if he didn't leave. I left with him, as my sister turned her rage on me for agreeing to leave with him. I was not leaving because I wanted to leave, but because my mother had said, "… take your family with you." In my mind, that was what she wanted and that was what I did.

We went back to his family's home. His parents had moved but his grandmother, his aunt, and her children had moved in. We stayed in the basement unit that we had when we were first married. I didn't stay there long. My husband was his usual abusive self and the first time that he hit me, I moved out and went to live with a cousin. I had an arrest warrant placed against him, but he left town.

Soon after, my in-laws were able to get custody of my sons and I was able to see them regularly. My oldest son had become very withdrawn because of the treatment that he had received at the children's home. I remember that on one visit, when I went to see them, my oldest son had a deep scratch on his face. When I inquired about the scratch, I was told that one of the other children had scratched him. However, my son said that one of the ladies scratched him and the scratch did look consistent with one that would have been done with long fingernails. When I asked him which lady scratched him, he said that she was not there. When my in-laws found out about the scratch, they decided to file for custody of the children and of course, I agreed to allow them to do so.

I managed to find a job as a shirt presser and the pay was enough for me to take care of me and my daughter. When my in-laws gained custody of my sons, my mother-in-law asked me to move in with them so that I could take care of them. They assured me that they had not heard from my husband since I'd pressed charges against him. By "mere coincidence," he showed up in the middle of the night about two or three weeks later. We talked for most of the night and, reluctantly, I agreed to try to make a new start "for the sake of the kids." I was involved in a relationship which I immediately broke off. If I was going to do this, I wanted to do it right.

By this time, my father-in-law was foreman on another construction site, so my husband had no problem getting a job. He did okay for a while, but would accuse me of being with any man that came to the house. The quartet group, that I mentioned earlier, still had rehearsals at his parents' home. Usually everyone (except my husband) would either be in the basement or in the kitchen on rehearsal night. On one occasion, my husband said, "You're probably laying with every man in the group except my father." My response was, "What's wrong with your father? Ain't he a man?" Of course the fight was on. I was tired of being afraid to move without knowing when he would go off. He was still sneaky about the fights. He would hit me with pillows with such force, it would knock me down. That was to ensure that that he didn't leave any marks on me.

Our relationship took another turn when he starting sleeping with the girl next door. The breaking point was not the affair. I could have cared less about that. It was when I found out that I was punishing my oldest son for not doing what I told him to do. If I called him to me, he would not come and often would not answer me when I called. I couldn't understand what was wrong until I decided to sneak upstairs to see what he was doing. Before I got halfway up, I heard my husband saying, "If you move, I'm going to beat you." I lit into him like somebody crazy. He had really crossed the line! Abusing me was bad enough, but not my children – or in this case, my child. I knew that I had to get away from there. My son was in danger. I was still working, but I was also pregnant again. How was I going to take care of three children and another one on the way? From that day, it was constant fighting. I told my in-laws what he was doing and they told him that if it happened again, he would have to leave. They had custody, so, I couldn't take them anywhere without their permission. I let it be known that everybody in the house would be responsible if something happened to any of my kids. Every week for me became a struggle. I started sleeping on the sofa. My husband would come in and fold up the sofa while I was laying on it. I decided to leave because I was planning to kill him and make it look like self-defense. For about two weeks, I would take extra clothes to work and leave them at my co-worker's house. I left when another co-worker let me stay with him and his wife. I told my mother-in-law that I was getting a protective order against my husband if he came anywhere near me or my job. Fortunately, he really didn't know that I was leaving. I reminded my mother-in-law that she was responsible for the safety of my oldest son.

Two weeks after I left, I found a room to rent. I took my oldest son to live with me to ensure that he was safe. I enrolled him into the "Head Start" program during the day and he loved it. I started saving all of my change if I broke a dollar. By the time I stopped work, I had enough to pay my rent until after I had the baby. I had planned on working until I had the baby. Unfortunately, I let my temper get the best of me when the owner of the cleaners decided to put us on "piece work" and pay us per shirt. The reason: we were not getting enough work done. The reason that we were not getting enough work done was because my co-worker would go home for lunch and would often not come back for two or more hours. I objected to being penalized for someone else's slack, especially when I would try to keep the machines running. The pressing machines required two people to operate them in order for us to meet a certain quota. Nonetheless, the owner didn't care that I would work the machines alone. He was looking only at losing customers if their shirts were not ready on time. I was not going to stand for a pay cut because of something that was out of my control. So, I told the owner that I was not coming back and that his taxes could take care of me (by this time, it was a little easier to get "public assistance"). True to my word, I quit. The owner called me several times but I refused to go back to work. Under these circumstances, it appeared that I was about to go down hill again. As long as I was working, I was pretty much at ease taking care of myself and my son. Now I had to be concerned about finding larger living quarters without the benefit of a job.

I was still going to church and learning more about God's way being better than my way. Yet, I continued doing things my way. I was a praiser but not committed to His way. I reinitiated the relationship that I was in before my husband and I had gotten back together, knowing that this was not God's will for me. **BUT GOD!!** In spite of the stupid decisions that I continued to make, God always made a way for me. I was, once again, sinking in sinful waters, but He did not let me drown.

For I am ready to fall;
And my sorrow is continually before me

~ Psalm 38:17~

CHAPTER SIXTEEN:
Taking the Low Road

Things were getting better. For a while, I was at peace. After I quit my job, I spent a lot of time at my mother's house. She had gotten married and we were slowly becoming like family again. She lived only two blocks away from where I lived and I would walk to her house just to get out of my room. My "daddy" had six children and a lot of grandchildren. We all got along fine. I was elated! There I was – grown and about to give birth to my fourth child before I'd ever called a man "daddy."

I began to settle down a little. I was able to see my two youngest children at church on Sundays. I'd sent word to my husband that I would have him arrested if he came anywhere near my home. Therefore, I didn't see him until I made a really bad decision to go to a surprise birthday party for his great aunt. As long as I had known him, he didn't have anything to do with her family. There were no known problems – just an age difference. I still had a good relationship with his cousin, so, when she invited me to the party and assured me that he didn't know about the party, against my better judgment, I decided to go. It was well until I began to say my goodnights. Just as I was leaving, my husband came in. Coincidence? NOT!! His cousin told me that she found out that his uncle (the wife beater) told him that I was there. Anyway, he spoke, I spoke and left. I had a cab waiting for me but, before I could get in and close the door, he ran out and forced his way into the cab. We argued and the cab driver didn't know what to do. My husband had my arm in such a tight grip that I thought that he would break it. He told the cab driver, I was drunk (I had not been drinking) and he was just making sure that I got home alright. As I began to protest, his grip got tighter.

Nobody said anything else until we reached my house. By then he had seized my purse and taken my key. I'd thought about screaming for help, but decided not to because he had my key. If I screamed, he could leave and come back. So, I decided to take my chances. I knew, that the couple who lived downstairs, were home and if bad came to worse, they would call the police.

As soon as we got into my room, he started arguing. I'd made up my mind that this was my chance to kill him and call it "self-defense." I almost tuned him out as I was trying to figure out how I was going to kill him. I knew that I would only get one chance so I had to take time to figure it out.

This is what I decided: I was living in a rooming house and all of my dishes and cooking utilities were in my room. The only problem was he was between me and the drawer where I kept my knives. He started looking through my belongings and I knew that I had to do something quick. I picked up my purse, explaining that I had to take my medicine. As I fumbled with the bottle, I asked him to look in the corner and get me a soda. He had a cup of soda sitting on the dresser. When he turned to get my soda, I dropped 2 of my pills in his cup. We argued more when I refused to sleep with him. I was careful to stand in front of his cup long enough for the pills to dissolve. I knew that they wouldn't kill him (they were prescription pain pills) but I prayed that he would fall asleep so that I could kill him. He kept arguing and I kept refusing to sleep with him. He was too smart to start a fight, knowing that there were other people in the house.

He picked up his cup and drank all of it in quick gulps. Then he laid spread eagle across my bed. He told me that if I wasn't going to sleep with him, I would just have to sit up all night. I said, "Fine", and sat down. When I was sure that he was asleep, I prepared to leave. I called a cab and he never moved. I went into the drawer and put my hand on my sharpest knife. At that very moment, I had a vision: I'm behind bars, with blood on the wall, getting ready to deliver my baby. The vision was just a quick flash. I could only think about one thing – how would I tell my children that I killed their father?

I shut the door, eased out of the room, and waited outside for my cab. By the time that it arrived, I was so exhausted that I was convinced that I was in labor. I told the driver to take me to the hospital. When I explained to the doctor that I had had a serious altercation with my husband, he said that I was not in labor but on the verge of a "breakdown." They sedated me and released me the next morning. I called the police and they took me home.

The tenants that lived downstairs told us that my husband left just before we arrived. They said that he had been walking around during the night and they had called the police. He told the police that he was my husband and I had left him there. Nonetheless, they made him leave because my neighbors had never seen him before. The police that took me home, gave me instructions for filing a stay away order.

It was around 10am Saturday morning when I went to bed. I woke up after 4pm to the sound of my door being forced open. It appeared that a family member had called and I was incoherent. My sister (one of daddy's daughters) had my oldest son and when someone else in the family told her that they had been trying to reach me all day, she sent her boyfriend to find out why I wasn't answering the phone. I heard my neighbor calling me and saying, "I know she's in there" and my sister's friend said, "I'm going to break it." I got to the door just as the lock began to break. My neighbor, who was an elderly woman, was looking like she was scared half to death. After a lot of confusion, I finally understood why they were trying to break in. Apparently, after the last phone call (I didn't remember receiving any phone calls), I had knocked the receiver off of the hook. My neighbor didn't know what to do since she didn't know my sister's friend. She was also concerned that something was wrong when I didn't answer her knock. What a day! I was finally able to convince everyone that I was okay. I really felt bad that my neighbor had to go through all that drama because of me. She seemed relieved that I was okay and told me not to worry about her.

A few hours later, at my mother's house, my family listened as I told them about the events that had occurred over the past twenty-four hours. My sister's boyfriend wanted to know where to find my husband. He said, "I'll kill him for you." As big as my husband was, this man was much bigger, but mostly muscle. He could have probably taken my husband out with little effort and would have if I had told him where he might find him. As tempting as it sounded, I didn't want anybody going to jail over this, so I didn't tell him where he might find my husband.

Another Child is Born

My baby was due in January. In November, the doctors told me that they would have to induce labor as soon as they thought the baby weighed enough. At my last prenatal visit, I was told that my antibodies were rapidly increasing, that I should expect a call if the results of my blood test showed a significant increase from the last test. I spent that weekend at my mother's house. On Monday morning, I received a call from the hospital. The doctor said that they had been trying to contact me all weekend. He instructed me to come to the hospital immediately. I took my time getting there. I even went shopping for baby things.

I arrived at the hospital after 1pm. The doctor had called at approximately 9a. As I was walking in, a doctor was walking out. He started to pass me and turned back to ask if I was Mrs. _____. I acknowledged that I was. He informed me that he had just put out a police report to have me picked up. I didn't believe him. He told me that he was going for lunch and would induce my labor when he returned. As I reached the check in desk, he called to the receptionist and told her to "Cancel the alert; Mrs. _____ just arrived." Was he serious??? The receptionist assured me that he was and that I could have been arrested and charged with child endangerment. Within a few hours, I was in labor and a few hours later – IT'S A BOY!!

By the time that I was fully alert, from the effects of the anesthesia, my new son had been taken to the nursery. It was a few hours before I could see him. All the other babies appeared to be asleep. He was kicking and screaming so loudly that his entire body was turning red. I stood there watching him (I was not allowed to go into the nursery to hold him) and said to myself, "He is going to be one mean little boy." I know that it was my fault. I was angry most of the entire duration of my pregnancy. I had no problem with "getting physical", even when I knew that I could not win. Before I left my husband, we'd had plenty of fights. I knew that I couldn't beat him, but I had to get at least one good lick in. My husband was always careful not to leave bruises on me, so he would often use pillows to hit me. The force behind those pillows was so great that I would almost always fall when I was hit. I remember one particular occasion when I called him an S.O.B. He hit me so hard that I bounced when I fell. I got up, kicked him and told him that he was still an S.O.B. Down I went again and got up again, trying to hit him, and repeated the same words. I was knocked down about four times. I was trying to hit him below the belt but he was too quick on his swing. He caught a couple of punches to the gut, but not enough to do any damage. He gave up after I told him that as long as I had breath to breathe, he would still be an S.O.B. He must have gotten tired because he just looked at me and called me a stupid B----.

He had the nerve to go to bed. What a fool! It was not long before he was asleep. I picked up a hammer and stood over him for a long time trying to convince myself to bust his head open. But, who would take care of my children, especially my oldest son, if I did that. At this point, I knew that I really had to leave.

There was another occasion that stands out in my mind as it relates to my anger and willingness to fight. While I was pregnant and working at the laundry, I got into a couple of scraps with my co-worker (the same man who let me live with him and his wife for a few weeks). He liked to tease people a lot – always joking, sometimes to the extreme. The first physical altercation occurred on one of those days when he went to the extreme. I was the butt of the joke. When I'd had enough, I warned him to leave me alone. Well, that warning just led to more jokes. I picked up a wooden clothes hanger and hit him until I drew blood (not much). He was still laughing and calling me crazy before he noticed that he was bleeding. Neither of us could believe that I'd hit him that hard.

About a month later, we got into an argument because he had not dumped a load of shirts that we were waiting to press. The boss cussed him out and he thought that I had told the boss that he was sleeping. Actually, he was "high" and sleeping, but I was not guilty of the charge. The argument became heated and he kept getting in my face. Not realizing my own strength, I literally picked him up and dumped him in the shirt bin. We could see nothing but his legs sticking up from the bin. That sobered him up!

Therefore, as I stood watching my baby boy kicking and screaming, I knew that I had, in the words of the older women, "marked him." I regretted not listening to the warning – "Be careful how you act when you are pregnant. Your baby will act the same way." I instinctively knew that I had "marked" my baby. Every time that I went to the nursery, he was kicking and screaming.

As expected, my baby had to receive blood transfusions before he was released from the hospital. However, he didn't have to stay as long as my other babies. He was home in approximately two weeks and I was so happy. He was a little spoiled because there were so many other children around when we visited my mother. Then, I moved into my mother's house when he was approximately three months old.

There I was again – living with my mother. This time, it was so much better. Her marriage was good for both of us. We actually began to bond. She was not just doing the motherly duty, she was being a mother and it really was good being with her. This time, I had a very large room and I only had two of my children with me – my oldest and my youngest. The middle children were with my in-laws and I could see them regularly.

The Devil Came Back

Soon after moving in with my mother, my husband came back to his parent's home. He had the nerve to come to "see" the baby. I made him wait outside until I brought the baby to the door. I wouldn't let him hold him. The visit was less than five minutes. Two days later, I went downtown to reactivate the stay away order. He reestablished his relationship with the girl that lived next door to them and started a new family. His mother allowed him to take my children to stay with him on weekends. I protested because it interfered with me seeing them on the weekends at church. In order to spite me, he decided to send the children to out of town relatives. Despite my in-laws having custody of the children, they said that my husband had rights and that they could not make him bring the children back. My daughter was sent to his biological mother and my son to her sister. Of course that put me in another bad state of mind. I vowed at that point that if I ever got them back again, no one would be able to take them away from me. During that time, I could only be happy that I still had my youngest and oldest sons with me. They both gave me comfort as I cared for them. My oldest got used to not being around my in-laws and my youngest was too young to know them. We attended the same church, but that was the only connection that we had with my in-laws.

With help of my new family, I managed not to go back into an ugly slump. I was depressed at times, but I managed to suppress it until I could deal with it. I continued to have migraine headaches and was sent to see a therapist. His solution to my problem was to prescribe tranquilizers. They did help to decrease the headaches, but I stopped taking them after about a month. After approximately two weeks of taking the medication, I knew when it was time to take one without having to look at a clock. I was not about to allow a drug to take over my life so I stopped taking the drug or going to the doctor that prescribed it.

It was as if Satan was trying destroy me in a more subtle way – get me hooked on drugs. **But God...** Drugging and drinking was not a problem that I, like some of my friends, would have to deal with. I'd seen too much drinking and the ill effects of it on too many people. I had too many friends who were dead or in jail due to the consequences of drugs. Because of the Lord's mercy, I did not have a desire for either alcohol or drugs. As previously mentioned, I tried drinking a few times, but it was not for me.

There were times when I felt completely washed out, **But God...** like the loving father that He is, continued to reach down to pick me up, no matter how many times I fell. I began to focus on being the best mother that I knew how to be. I was increasing my personal time of devotion and learning more of how to accept God's forgiveness for the part that I played in making a mess out of my life.

"Human brutes, like other beasts, find snares and poison in the provision of life, and are allured by their appetites to their destruction. "

Jonathan Swift
(Anglo-Irish[1] satirist, essayist, poet and Dean of St. Patrick's Cathedral, Dublin)

CHAPTER SEVENTEEN:
Small But Significant Changes

lthough I thought things were getting better for me, I
still had some major challenges. I knew that I had to
make some changes in my life, but seriously, I didn't
want to change every-thing in my life that needed to
be changed. I liked doing some of those things. Nonetheless,
change came, in spite of what I wanted. The first significant
change was definitely an unwelcome one. My health began to
fail. I was sick, often. The migraines were increasing in
frequency and intensity.

I was diagnosed with ulcers when my baby was
approximately 5 months old. The doctors kept insisting that I
had to be drinking. That was the furthest thing from the truth
unless you wanted to count RC Cola. I didn't like alcoholic
beverages (not even beer). I hadn't had a beer since my
daughter was three months old (after my sons were taken
from me). I had tried a few times, but really didn't like the
stuff. When my daughter was almost a year old, I received a
bottle of bourbon from my boss (at the laundry) as a
Christmas gift. Christmas Eve was very difficult for me that
year. It was just me and her. I was wrapping gifts and feeling
sorry for myself. I decided to take a drink. I poured out a
good bit (more soda than bourbon) and before I could drink
more than a few sips, I knocked it over on one of the gifts.
That bothered me so much that I put the bottle away. It was
good that I didn't drink more. If I had, I would hate to think

what could have happened later that night/early the next morning.

I was living with my cousin. She and her kids went to visit my aunt in New York. She told me that her husband would be spending Christmas with his family and I would have the apartment to myself for a few days. I decided to sleep in her room that night. I awakened in the early hours of the morning to the sound of gun shots. My cousin's husband was standing in front of the mirror with a gun. He was so drunk, he thought that he was trying to shoot someone that was trying to shoot him. He didn't even know where he was. Somehow, I managed to talk him into putting the gun down. When he finally realized where he was and what he had done, he sobered up quickly. He was so afraid of what my cousin would do about him drinking, he wanted me to tell her that someone was trying to break into the apartment. Dumb! I got my daughter and went into the kid's bedroom, but I couldn't sleep. I stayed in that room until I heard him leave. I was so grateful that I had enough thought to stay calm. If I had awakened in a confused state of mind, my daughter and I might have gotten shot.

The next time that I tried a strong drink was after I had been diagnosed with ulcers. Therefore, the ulcers could not have possibly been caused by alcohol. That last drink had not been much. My baby boy was probably around seven or eight months old. I was playing cards with my sister and some friends. They had drinks set up, so, I decided to drink a couple of RCs laced with bourbon. I know that I didn't drink much because I had to take care of my kids. However, I got so sick the next morning that I could hardly function. I would be clear enough to attend to the baby when he needed attention, but as soon as I would finish with him, the room would start spinning. Fortunately, my oldest son was with my sister's children most of the day. The alternating between a spinning room and a caring mother continued well into the night. The day after, I made a solemn promise to God – "If You get me out of this, You will never have to worry about me taking another drink." Within a couple of hours, I was fine. I have kept that promise. As for the cause of the ulcers – they were peptic ulcers caused by stress. The condition became worse and I would really get sick. When there was an onset of the migraine headaches, it would trigger nausea which would activate the symptoms of the ulcers. It was not unusual for me to literally pass out anywhere.

There were other changes that were on the positive side. I'd started working on some weekends (child care). My nieces would babysit my children when I worked. I found an apartment nearby. My oldest son was doing well in Head Start and I was beginning to settle down a little. By this time, I had broken the relationship that I was in and started dating someone at the church that I attended. He was really nice to me and to my children. We saw a lot of each other (mostly on weekends). It became obvious that we were getting serious about each other. However, I was not interested in being too serious. I had made a promise to myself that I would never date a single man. As we learned more about each other, he told me that he was married but separated from his wife since the first year of their marriage. He had a son who was approximately nine years old. When he told me this, I had no problem with it at all. "The better for me," I thought to myself. At some point, his son came to live with him. The children got along well together.

Neither Rain Nor Snow...

When my children were in their late teens, I would tell them stories about the hard times that we had to endure. But, there were also stories that included good memories, even from the hard times. The following is one of those stories:

One winter, during the time that my husband and I were dating, it snowed and almost shut down the city. No public transportation was running. My friend lived approximately three miles from me. We talked on the phone that Friday evening (when he would normally come to visit me). There was three feet of snow on the ground and it was still snowing. Of course, I mentioned that I would miss seeing him and said something about not getting any moon pies that night. Later that evening, he was knocking at my door with a box of moon pies in his hand. He had walked the three miles just to bring me moon pies and then had to walk back home. I was absolutely amazed that he cared enough to see that I got those moon pies. My children were also amazed every time they heard the story. It was those types of things that he would do that drew me closer to him. He didn't have much, but if I wanted something and he could get it, he would.

Straddling the Fence

As much as I liked this man, there were things that caused me a good deal of discomfort concerning our relationship. I was also becoming more serious about my relationship with God. I was a very serious woman of praise, but had no power to live seriously as a praiser. I had grown but not enough to grasp the true reality of praise. There were many time when I told myself that I would have to stop dating this man. We dated for five years before we were married, and for at least three of those years, I repented more times than I can recall. I wanted to be saved, but I was not willing to give up my relationship with this man. I told myself every time that we were intimate, that it would be the last time. I told him the same, but it never worked out the way I'd planned. It was especially bad as the years continued. I would have an emotional experience every New Year and promise God that I would be celibate. That promise would not last more than two weeks.

But God continued to watch over me and continued to provide for me. In spite of my blatant disobedience, He began turning things around for me. Some of the changes were readily accepted. Others caused me a lot of anxiety. My Pastor would preach messages that felt as if she was throwing fire and brimstone straight from hell into my chest. Over and over, I would go home and repent, but then I was back in that man's arms. I could not or would not resist the fires of temptation. Again and again, I found myself enjoying the pleasures of sin. The Strange thing about all of this was that it was this man that was mostly responsible for the conflict. We would spend hours talking about the scriptures or the things of God. He had such an influence over me in all of his God-like behaviors. He was kind and sincere, yet both of us were sincerely wrong and on our way to hell by way of the church.

But God ... had a plan. I was really trying to get myself together. I kept hearing messages that I knew were specifically for me. Church was becoming one of the brightest spots in my life. I became very involved with the work of the church. I was an usher, a choir member, and eventually the church secretary. When I think back, I think that becoming the church secretary was a major part of God's plan to draw me closer to Him. My pastor was an encourager. She was a warrior in the pulpit and out. However, she was very gentle in teaching me on a personal level, while I served as her secretary. Under the guise of discussing "church business", she taught me many invaluable lessons regarding real service to/for God. Sometimes, we would talk late into the night and often. During those talks, she would start out talking about church matters, in general, but she would always manage to get on a particular topic regarding godly living. I fell for the "bait" every time. As the years went by, she and I would discuss many issues wherein she was telling me, without actually saying the words, that if I knew what God was saying, then I would be held accountable for the change which was needed in my life. I'm happy to report that her teaching was not all in vain.

Therefore, if any man is in Christ, he is a new creation; old thing have passed away; behold, all things have become new.

2 Corinthians 5:17

CHAPTER EIGHTEEN:
Changed

During the five years that my husband and I dated, I obtained my GED, took a course in stenography and got a job with the Department of Army, during the Vietnam Era. I was also able to obtain a house through Public Housing. Although, I was becoming financially independent, I was struggling to make one check last to the next one. Little by little, my government benefits were terminated and I discovered that it cost more to work than to say at home. However, I didn't let that deter me. I somehow knew that I would be able to take care of my family. I continued to have migraine headaches, but I tried to keep my stress levels to a minimum. My children were in a good child care program and basically things were changing for the better.

What was not changing was the fact that I was still involved with someone who was not my husband. I was still struggling with my spirituality or lack thereof. So many times I would find myself stressing over my sin. I heard the word and it was eating me up. Scripture was repeated over and over in my mind, i.e., "you can't be just a hearer of the Word, you must be a doer of the Word"; "He that knows the will of the master and does not do it shall be beaten with many stripes. And if he does not know and does things that deserve punishment, he will be beaten with a few stripes"; "Get your house in order." (Quotes are paraphrased) I really had a war going on inside of me. I prayed and fretted. I guess that at some point, God got tired of me praying for help and then doing the same things the same ways, getting the same result. It was during one of those times when I was praying, I clearly heard the Holy Spirit speak to my mind – "Marry the man or keep him out of your bed." That was not exactly what I wanted to hear. I wasn't ready to commit to marriage. I had promised myself that I would never marry again. That was the only reason that I had not divorced my husband – to keep me ineligible. No, no, no, no!! No marriage!!! **But God....**

I don't remember how we started discussing marriage. It may have been one of those times when we would try to limit our physical contact, knowing that it would not last. The bottom line was we both loved the Lord and wanted to do the right thing. Of course, with the subject of marriage, came the subject of divorce. Neither of us were financially able to file. So I thought that was an excuse. Not! We decided to check around to see what the rates for a lawyer would be. I remembered that as a child, we lived in an apartment over a law office. I looked up the lawyer and talked with him. It turned out to be easier than I had anticipated. Within a few months both of us were divorced and were making plans to get married.

When we made it known that we were going to get married, the debate about the divorce and remarriage got started. I know that I had biblical grounds for divorce and believed that he did too. I had an aunt to tell me that even if I got a divorce, I could not remarry and be saved. Something or somebody was wrong. I knew that I heard "get married or...." I was becoming confused. Then I remembered a conversation that I'd had with a pastor from Ohio who would visit us regularly. She was a strict, no nonsense preacher. The conversation had come up about remarriage after divorce. I voiced my opinion that it really didn't make any difference to me because it would take "God, Himself to speak directly to me before I would ever marry anyone else." Her response was "with God, nothing is impossible." Well, I know what I heard and, if it was the Holy Spirit that had spoken to me, then it was God. Therefore, I proceeded with plans to get married. We set a date as soon as our divorces were final.

We Changed My Name

We did not want an elaborate ceremony, nor did we plan to have a reception. The only stipulation that really mattered was that our outfits would be color coordinated. He had a suit that was cornflower blue. I planned to get a dress or suit the same color. I could not find that color in any of the stores. Two weeks before the wedding, I still did not have a dress/suit. One day, I went to a ten dollar store to get something (I'm not sure what) and saw a two piece skirt and top in the color that I had been looking for. It was by no means as nice as I wanted, but I bought it anyway in the event that I could not find anything else. Well, I wore that suit for my wedding! I didn't care as long as it was cornflower blue. I estimated that my entire outfit had not cost me more than a hundred dollars. It really didn't matter. Our wedding day was on a Sunday. We went to my father's church and he performed the ceremony after his morning worship service. Then we went to our church take part in our Church Anniversary celebration, which started that day. Most of the members were not aware that we had gotten married until our pastor made the announcement. **Oh, happy day.**

We did not go anywhere for our honeymoon. Nothing was different except that, for the first time, we spent the night together. We both went to work the next day. He moved into my house and we became a family. His son continued to live with his mother and visited with us on weekends. I didn't feel any different, physically or spiritually. My name and marital status was changed and I no longer felt guilty when we were intimate. Other than that, I was the same. I don't know what I really expected. Maybe, I thought that I would be filled with the Holy Spirit and began speaking in a heavenly language the next Sunday following my wedding. It didn't happen then or the next Sunday or for many Sundays to come. We settled into a routine and things were good. I found out that there were more changes that had to take place on the inside of me.

I Changed My Job

When I got married, I had been employed with the Department of Army for approximately one year. My supervisor was ex-military, very demanding, and prejudice. After almost two years, I quit the job because she had so offended me and I threatened to slap her if she ever raised her voice at me again. She had a way ranting and yelling when she was upset about something. The Captain and the Colonel assigned to our office would allow her to throw temper tantrums with them but I would not tolerate it. Before the incident in which I threatened her, I had expressed my dislike about her yelling at me on more than one occasion. This last event was accompanied by her throwing a stack of papers on my desk. As I was trying to keep my anger from getting the best of me, she came back and snatched the papers and told me that there was nothing else for me to do, so I might as well leave. I asked if she was granting me leave and she said "no." Therefore I refused to leave. When the Colonel came in, she went into his office and shut the door. Obviously, she told him that I threatened to slap her. When she came out of the office, she informed me that the Colonel wanted to see me.

The Colonel and I talked about the incident and he admitted that she was difficult to get along with. He suggested that I would just allow her to rant and ignore her until she settled down. I informed him that her behavior toward me was unacceptable and that I would not allow her to stand in my face while she ranted. He also suggest that I take the rest of the afternoon off. I again refused to leave unless they were going to grant me administrative leave. Actually, I wanted to leave, but I chose to stay – not because they wouldn't give me leave, but because I knew that she could not stand the idea that I had the audacity to challenge her. I left at my regular time and wished them both a good night.

The next day, I turned in my resignation. My supervisor did not know that I had done this until she received the papers from the personnel office. She was indignant but calm. "Why wasn't I told that you were resigning?" she asked. "If you know that I'm resigning, you must have been told." I replied. She wanted to know why I didn't tell her. I responded that I wasn't required to tell her. She had the nerve to ask why I was leaving. I let her know that I was trying to avoid problems for both of us. On my last day, I left with my usual "Have a good evening."

I had only been married for approximately three months when I quit my job. Knowing that my husband couldn't afford the full responsibility of taking care of his new family, I immediately started looking for another job. It took about three months, but I landed a good job with the telephone company. I continued to have migraines. Therefore, I missed a lot of work days. When I worked for the Department of Army, not much was said, as long as I had a doctor's excuse. It was not that easy with the telephone company. I eventually lost that job due to excessive absenteeism. I was asked to resign. I refused because I needed to be able to draw unemployment. If I was laid off, that would not be a problem, or so I thought.

My unemployment benefits were denied because my employers reported that I was fired for "disorderly conduct." What??? Since when was being sick considered to be disorderly conduct? I appealed the decision. I won, but I won only because of my supervisor. She had not been informed of the unemployment denial and the pending hearing. I just happened to receive a call from her which was not work related. At the end of our conversation, I told her that I would see her at the upcoming hearing. She knew nothing about it but assured me that she would be there.

On the day of the hearing, I arrived to see a group of people from the telephone company that I didn't know. The proceeding began and my supervisor was not there. The representative of the phone company began to read from prepared documents, indicating that I was habitually late, that I had been warned on several occasions and that other employees were required to do my work. Just before I was called to respond to the charges, my supervisor walked in, apologizing for being late. Every one of the telephone company representatives looked absolutely shocked as she identified herself as my supervisor. Questions, from the panel, resulted in several illegal actions being revealed: First, my supervisor was not issued a notice of the hearing; secondly, someone other than my supervisor had signed off on the charges when the document should have been signed by her; thirdly, none of her superiors had obtained a report from her regarding my employment. She informed the panel that there were records regarding my illness and that there were days when I came to work and she knew that I was sick. She also informed the panel that when I was at work, I was often given work of the other employees who could not keep their files up to date and that I was an excellent worker. Case closed – I won! And – all that she said was true.

So, there I was again – unemployed and trying to make ends meet with my husband's salary and my unemployment benefits. It was a struggle and I realized that things could have been worse.

BUT GOD ... continued to look beyond my faults and He supplied our need.

He Changed My Life

Gradually, I began to notice subtle changes about myself. Small changes that over time made major differences in the way I looked at life in general and the way I became aware of my need for the move of the Holy Spirit's control over all of my life. The anointing in the Holy Spirit came at a most unusual time for me. I yet marvel at the way God chooses to do what He does in my personal relationship with Him. Certainly, according to my way of thinking, I was not ready for the gift of the Holy Spirit with the evidence of speaking in other tongues. I am constantly reminded that when we tell God to have His way in our lives, we had better mean it. I received that marvelous gift at a time when I least expected.

I will never forget that day – the first Sunday in February, 1971. We had been married approximately one and a half years. It was "Men's Day" at our church. For some unknown reason, I couldn't seem to get myself and the children ready for church in a timely manner. My husband was ready and did what he could to help out. Finally, seeing that we were going to miss the bus that would get us to church on time, he became a little impatient with my pace and kept telling me to hurry. I became irritated and told him that if he was in such a hurry, to leave. My tone was not nice. When I finally came downstairs, he was gone. I was past irritated. I was mad! How dare he leave me with the children??? It wasn't like I hadn't gotten to church without him before. By the time I got to church, it was almost time for the choir (of which I was a member) to sing. I slipped into the choir stand and became angrier each time that I looked toward my husband who did not seem to notice. As the service proceeded, I kept thinking about how I was going to "tell him off" when we got home. That never happened. When the guest preacher began to speak, my focus was immediately turned to him and the message. The message was entitled "Get Off the Fence." It seemed as though I was taken to an unknown level of worship and somewhere between the end of the message and the altar call, I was lifted to new heights that I had never known. Apparently, I had been "slain in the Spirit" because when I became aware of my natural surroundings again, I was laid out in front of the altar. What an awesome, unexplainable moment!

I knew that a significant change had been made in my life. The way that I can best express my change is in the words of the song "Changed", by Tramaine Hawkins:

> *A change, a change has come over me. He changed my life and now I'm free. He washed away all my sin and he made me whole. He washed me white as snow. He changed my life complete and now I sit at His feet. To do what must be done; I'll work and work until He comes.*
> **A wonderful change has come over me**
> *I'm not what I want to be. I'm not what I use to be. I'm not the same way.*
> **Thank God - Thank God! I'm so glad he changed me**
> *He changed my walk, He changed my talk, He changed my life he even changed my soul.*
> **A wonderful change has come over me**

I've come a long way, in Jesus, I've come a long way, in Christ. I've come a long way, Thank God! A wonderful change has come over me! Over the years, low self-esteem was changed to a total dependence on God, whom I allowed to take His rightful place as the "Head of my life." Willful disobedience was kicked to the curb and a "do-right" mind took its rightful place. That first Sunday in February, 1971 was definitely a turning point that has brought me from a horrible place to a place of gratefulness. No, life has not been perfect and it will not be until I see Jesus face to face.

But God... has shown me a great light in His Son, Christ Jesus. He has been with me through every storm, and there have been many. Because of the change, I have learned (and I'm still learning) how to apply God's word to my circumstances. He sent His Word to heal me and I stand on every promise that He gives me.

I'm not going back,
I'm moving ahead;
Here to declare to You,
My past is over in You.
All things are made new,
Surrendered my life to Christ.
I'm moving forward.
You make all things new and
I will follow You forward.

Israel Houghton – Moving Forward

CHAPTER NINETEEN:

Moving Forward

It was not difficult for us to make adjustments as we blended our family. The children were already getting along before we were married. However, we did need a larger house so that we could be comfortable.

Our first Christmas together was really good, except for the planned Christmas dinner. I invited some of my husband's family for dinner and in my nervousness, it ended up being an absolute flop. I wanted to have dinner ready when they arrived so that there would be no need for a lot of traffic in my small kitchen. Well, it didn't go so smoothly. First, I forgot about the corn bread until almost the time for our family's arrival. In my haste, I forgot to add the eggs to the batter. The bread was "Bricks Ville." Fortunately, I had some dinner rolls. Secondly, it started snowing at a fast rate and the family was more than an hour late, which required that I reheat some of the food. I put the turkey back in the oven to warm. It was the last thing to go on the table. When I put it on the platter, the platter broke in two. For me, that was the last straw. I was visibly upset. I felt like a complete failure who had just made a horrible first impression as a hostess. To make matters worse, it was snowing so hard that we had to rush through dinner so that my family could head back home. I felt as though I would never get over the embarrassment, but I did.

Approximately a year after we married, my husband was called into the preaching ministry. After his ordination, some of the members decided that I needed to change my image. "I should wear hats; I should look like a preacher's wife." Of course, I didn't agree. I seldom wore a hat and had no intention of allowing those busy bodies to tell me how to look like a preacher's wife. Make no mistake, considering that our finances were meager, I knew how to dress on our low income without looking like I was destitute. In some cases, I dressed just as well as some of the female preachers, if not better. I knew how to shop at some of the best stores in DC without paying outrageous prices. Of course lay-away and sales were absolutely necessary pluses. Therefore, as it related to dressing, the only person I had to be concerned about was me. I did take into consideration that women at my church were under a denominational dress code and for the most part, I did adhere to it. However, I was instrumental (along with our Assistant Pastor's wife) in changing some of the rules. I wore small items of jewelry and light makeup, as well as some fine shoes. Shoes were my thing. When I was working, I normally would purchase at least two or three pair of shoes a month. I may not have worn the name brands, but I did wear some "glad rags" on most Sundays and special occasions.

Two weeks before our second Christmas, I had a miscarriage. The pregnancy had only been confirmed four days prior to the miscarriage. When the doctor confirmed that I was pregnant, he put me on immediate bed rest, to no avail. Although, I never felt any discomfort, I was hospitalized for two days. During that time, I kept thinking that the medication that my doctor had given me to prevent the loss, actually caused it. However, I didn't let it bother me too much. I was learning to accept what God allowed.

In August of 1971, we moved from the projects into our house. It was not what we wanted, but we had to take what we could afford. It's a very small house, but we managed. To this day, I call it my "cracker box", but trust me when I say that I am grateful, I am truly grateful. I thank God for my "cracker box." We made it work. We had/have a roof over our heads. God has blessed and continues to bless us to always have enough food and clothing. He provided for our need, even as He promised. We had some good times and some struggling times. Through it all, I was learning to trust God more and to take Him at His word, even when I couldn't understand some of His methods.

Life has its irony. We thought that we were settling into a very nice neighborhood. The residents on our street were mostly middle age to seniors. Our street was very quiet and clean. However, we soon realized that we were surrounded with drugs and a high rate of crime. We couldn't go two blocks in either direction without seeing and feeling the effects. Some of those effects trickled back to our street. Within a year, there were quite a few young adults and unruly teenagers in our area. They consisted of kids who had been away to college or those who were new to the area. The kids on our street were, for the most part, well mannered. That was not always the case with those who lived in the nearby vicinity.

We thought that we were moving to an area where our children would be safe and the schools would provide a better education. That all changed when our children started Jr. High school. My husband and I thought that we were doing a pretty good job of teaching our children right standards and morals. We **took** them to church and taught them the importance of living as a Christian. I'm saddened to report that they were learning more from the street life than from us. It is true – you do reap what you sow, even when you stop sowing bad seeds. The devil slipped in the back door. My husband and I found out, too late, that we were spending so much time in church that we were not spending enough quality time with our children. **But God ....** All is not lost. The seeds of righteousness have already been planted. God will do for them, what he did for me. He promised that my household (my family) will be saved – all of them!

Throughout the 1970's, I continued to have migraines, but not as severe. I obtained a part time job with the Department of Army (US Military Finance). I was offered a full time job almost simultaneously with being offered a job with the US Secret Service (a job for which I did not apply). The grade/pay was highest for the Secret Service so I accepted the job with that agency. God was blessing me physically, financially, and most certainly spiritually. That is not to say that everything was as I thought it should have been. It seemed as though every time we thought that we finally had established our footing, some devastating circumstance would break in like an intruder in the night. **But God....** Always my sustainer, strength, and joy. When I felt like I would lose it, He kept me. When I thought that I was too weak to keep going, He gave me strength. When I had to cry over disappointments, He gave me joy and a determination to push forward.

Singing in the Rain

In the early seventies, I and one of my co-workers decided to take night courses (stenography) at a local high school. Our teacher, who was also an evangelist, spent more time telling us about her marvelous pastor and her wonderful church than she did teaching us. She would invite us to attend the worship services at her church. Finally, my co-worker, who is also one of the best friends I've ever had, and I decided to visit (just to stop the teacher from asking us). I will never forget that Sunday! First of all, the singing and preaching left nothing to be desired. Yes, the teacher/evangelist was right – her pastor really knew how to handle the Word. Secondly, I had been laying before the Lord, for more than a week, regarding a specific problem that I was experiencing. During the week before the Sunday that we visited the church, the Lord had begun to show me some things, in dreams, regarding the problem. During the altar call, the pastor called me out and asked if he could pray for me. Although I was usually a little leery about strangers calling me out, I did not hesitate to go to the altar. Before the pastor prayed, he said some things in my ear that only God could have spoken to him. He even used some of the same phrases that God had spoken to my spirit during that past week. God had used this stranger to confirm His Word to me. God had sent me to the right place to receive the right word for me on that Sunday. The message was titled "This Too Shall Pass." I thank God for that word so many times, even to this day. I know that no matter how hard the task may get or how strong the winds of opposition may blow, it will pass because God said so.

Again, I cannot say that from that Sunday, things were always as I thought that they should be. However, I can say that I was beginning to use different weapons. The winds of opposition kept blowing. It seemed as though there was one storm after another and I would be reminded that every storm would pass. As I previously mentioned, I was a praiser and, by this time in my life, I believed that I could praise my way through anything. I knew the value of prayer as I had never known before. Although prayer did not always change my situation, it often changed how I responded to negative circumstances. In addition, I was in that little store front where there was always good singing. I loved quartet singing, but in the seventies, my musical focus was more on contemporary gospel music. So many of those songs would fit into who I was and what I believed. As I reflect, it seemed as though God had a song in my heart to meet every situation. It didn't matter if I was happy or sad, songs would saturate my spirit throughout each day with very few exceptions. On those occasions when I could not feel a song in my heart, I knew that I was in trouble, spiritually. It was during those "no song" days that I would cry out to God like a lost child searching for its parent. "God, where are You?" He would minister to me in a very personal way – just me and Him. But, instead of a song, He would take me to His Word to show me that ministry through His Word was more powerful than a song. I've had many days when I had to cry real tears. **But God....** He taught me how to sing in the rain. Although I could not carry a straight tune, I could sing myself happy. I would bask in the music of the songs and allow His Spirit to completely satisfy me.

I press toward the mark for the prize of the high calling of God in Christ Jesus.

~ Philippians 3:14 ~

Chapter Twenty:
Take Me Higher Lord

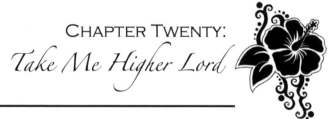

When I got saved (for real, for real), I promised God that I would do whatever He wanted me to do. I would often pray, "Take me higher Lord." I would sing songs that had the implication of going higher with the Lord. Little did I realize, at the time, what I was really asking Him to do. I thought that I was merely asking the Lord to draw me closer to Him. I did not consider that pressing toward "a higher calling in Him" would mean that He would call me to teach or preach His Word. Although I was doing some teaching (Sunday School and a little teaching after our midweek prayer service), I certainly would have never imagined that I would be preaching.

In the late seventies, I received the "call" to the preaching ministry. I didn't want to preach. I didn't believe that I was qualified. My calling came as I was reading/studying the Book of Jeremiah. I could not believe it! I struggled with it. I made excuses, all to no avail. God had already shaped my destiny. He did not need my permission. I finally understood that my arms were too short to box with God. I kept getting stuck on the passage in Jeremiah that said, "… be not dismayed at their faces, lest I confound thee before them." (Chapter 2:17). Since I had promised God that I would go where He leads, I reluctantly surrendered. I answered the call and became satisfied with the idea that God would trust me to carry His Word.

Although I received my calling in the latter part of the 1970's, it was a few months before I was convinced that I had received the call. I had said, "Yes" to the Lord, but I had not taken any steps to move until I was, yet again, "slain in the Spirit." Seldom would I go down to the floor, but when I did, I would get up with a sense of going to a new level in my relationship with Christ. Such was the occasion when I found myself crying out to the Lord, "Yes, I'll go." It had been a public affirmation, so there was no turning back. It was in August of 1980.

It was a tremendous struggle trying to prepare my initial sermon. It wasn't that God wasn't speaking. I wasn't listening. Oh, I heard what He said the first time that He said it. But, being my usual self, I wanted a catchy sermon – not some "fire and brimstone message." I went weeks trying to get the "right message" and nothing was coming together. Two weeks before the date of my initial message, I still did not have one. Wrong! I did have it, but kept rejecting it. My last attempt at trying to find the right message ended with me not being able to read the pages in front of me. The pages in the Bible became two black pages. I quickly closed the book and said "Okay, Lord, have it your way." I was so nervous that I was shaking. The next day, I began to prepare the message that God had given me in the beginning. I was licensed to the ministry in January of 1981. The subject of the message: "Sin, It's a Crying Shame." Almost immediately, I was regularly being asked to speak at our local churches, and I was also evangelizing out of town as often as I could accommodate the requests.

The Overseer of our church wanted to elevate me to the position of Elder within the first six months after I was licensed. Our Bishop agreed, but I was uneasy. It was the custom, in our church, that a minister be "proven" for a period of one year before being elevated to a higher position. At my insistence, although the intent to elevate me was made known during our Holy Convocation, I was not officially elevated until I had served for one year. I felt that God was pleased with the decision. I had a firm understanding that higher heights in Him also required deeper depths in Him. There was so much to learn.

I was an eager student. However, I couldn't seem to juggle my time so that I wouldn't feel overwhelmed. As for the message materials, I knew that God was speaking. Most of my sermons came at unexpected times and were almost always dealing with a need for change – not quite fire and brimstone, but I often felt as though I couldn't get through a sermon without a stern warning regarding our walk with the Lord. I later came to appreciate the fact that God would choose me – the biggest sinner that I had ever known. The sermons would always cause me to take a look at my walk so that I could see what things needed to be changed in my life.

The Devil Got in the Mix

Just as I thought that things were working out well, my family came under attack. As my children became adults, they were doing their own thing. Like chips off of the old block, they stopped going to church, not wanting to have anything to do with church. The one that did stay in the church was only there physically – talking the talk, but not walking the walk – like the church folk who wore two hats. Nonetheless, I continue to pray that one day, they will completely surrender their lives to Jesus as they come to the knowledge of the Truth. In the meanwhile, I let them know that there is nothing that they could ever do to stop me from loving them, partly because they are my children and partly because I know that my heavenly Father never stopped loving me, in spite of my disobedience. I can only believe that He will draw them to Him as He drew me to Him.

In the mid 1980's, my husband made a devastating announcement that struck a blow so hard that I wanted to leave him. My heart was absolutely broken. We had been in ministry together for so long that I couldn't imagine that he would ever choose to walk away. He had become the Assistant Pastor of our church and I was the Youth Pastor. He didn't leave me physically, but at the time, I felt as though he might as well had. Since he didn't leave me, I decided to leave him. How could he have made such a decision without talking with me before he decided to join another denomination?? I could see Satan's strategy right away. We really loved each other. We were so in tune that we seldom had an argument. When we dressed for church, he would be in one room and I would be in another and, most of the time, we would come out color coordinated without planning. We were a good fit for each other until he decided to change his way of thinking as it related to Christianity. He switched over to Jehovah's Witnesses, a group that we had talked about on many occasions, as it related to the differences in our beliefs and theirs. Then, behind my back, without any discussion, he joined them. I was devastated.

I moved out of our bedroom, planning to move out of the house when I could find a place to move. I spent a lot of time, trying to figure out how I could afford to move into an apartment. It would be just me, so I thought that I could find something. I thought about renting a room from someone. Every thought that I had didn't feel right. I couldn't figure it out until the morning that the Holy Spirit interrupted my thoughts. "Let the unbeliever depart." I was so taken aback that I answered (out loud), "I'm not no unbeliever!" The Holy Spirit responded, "Then, where are you going?" That was the end of it. I had nothing to say and He said no more.

Nonetheless, I was still upset with my husband. I remained in the other bedroom. I continued to cook and clean. I was cordial toward him. He gave me my space for a while and then tried to get me to understand his reasoning for the change that he had made. We could never get very far in our discussion because we would hit an area where we could never agree. It was a complete impasse. On one such discussion, he became so adamant that he began banging on the table and raising his voice, "I'm a Jehovah's Witness and I'm going to stay a Jehovah's Witness!" It was so out of character for him to act like that! I responded, "I'm Pentecostal and I'm going to stay Pentecostal and may the best God win!" End of discussion.

The next day, during my prayer time, I, again, saw clearly what was happening. Divide and conquer has always been the enemy's strategy. Well, I decided that it wouldn't work if I had anything to say about it. This was not one of the times that my impulses would have me make another bad decision. Therefore, I said to God, "This is Yours. I can't handle it. He's in Your hands." From that day, I decided to accept what God allowed. If He didn't change the situation, I knew that I couldn't. Yet, something that God had said to me a few years prior to this change in my husband, kept coming back to my mind – "I will use you to get through to your husband." I didn't know what it meant then and I still don't. When I last asked God to explain how He would use me and what I was supposed to do, He simply said, "Just live right and do your part." It has been more than twenty years and I'm still waiting. I do the best that I know how to be a good wife and I believe that he is doing his best to be a good husband. It is true – love covers a multitude of faults. He has his and I certainly have mine. But, through all of this, our love for each other grows stronger. These are some of the best times of our lives together.

Me and My Mother

My mother and I had become very close. Her marriage was the beginning of a great relationship between us. My marriage and subsequent life of total commitment to Christ was the beginning of a marvelous relationship with Him (Christ). Both my mother and I were more spiritually mature. Both of us became chosen vessels as evangelists. It seemed that we were not only mother and daughter; we became more like sisters. We shared almost everything with each other. Our churches were closely connected. Therefore, we were often in fellowship with each other's churches. Sometimes, we would go out as a preaching team. Other times, we would support one another when one of us had a speaking engagement. Our latter years were some of the best years of our lives as mother and daughter. My mother and I would talk extensively about anything – except my childhood. One evening, we were talking about some of my accomplishments. My mother suddenly became very quiet. After a brief moment, she told me that she was so very proud of me and that she knew that some of the things that I had done as a child were her fault and that she was very sorry. No explanation was given and none was needed. At that moment, I felt as though I had been given a million dollars (or at least what I thought how having a million dollars would feel). There was no doubt that my mother loved me and I love her. Satan thought that he had destroyed both of us, **But God...** loved the hell out of us so that we could love each other and then show others that God and love indeed covers a multitude of faults.

My Son Came Home!

There was more good news!! As God was taking me higher, He was also working things out for me at times and in ways that I did not expect. In 1982, my second son, whom I had not seen for seventeen years, called me just before the Thanksgiving Holidays, and we were reunited. I threw one of the biggest Thanksgiving Day celebrations ever (even though it was two weeks before Thanksgiving Day). I invited so many people to my "cracker box" that they had to come in shifts. "Come celebrate with me; my son is home!" He was my son, whom my ex-husband had sent to his aunt who lived in another state. This was one of his hateful ways to spite me. I had come close to finding him on a few occasions, but as soon as his aunt found out that I was getting close to finding him, she would move to another location. When she died, someone told my son how to contact me. Seventeen years! Grown, in the military, with a wife and son – coming home to mom! When he called me, he didn't have to tell me who he was. When he asked for me by name, my instincts kicked in and I knew that it was my son on the other end of the phone connection. **Oh happy Thanksgiving Day!**

I went to the bus station to pick up my children on the day that they came home. I saw my grandson before I saw my son and knew him the instant that I saw him jump off the bus. Except for skin tone, he was just like his daddy. He was three years old and stole my heart immediately. I cannot explain how my heart felt when I saw my son and his wife. I was so happy, words cannot describe.

Just before Christmas, of the same year, I drove to North Carolina to be with my son and family for the weekend. I wanted to be sure that I saw them for the holidays. It was a very good weekend. I got to enjoy them in a family setting. I also met my daughter-in-law's mother, who surprised them and also drove down that weekend. I had a wonderful time with my grandson who had a special way of teasing/tricking us, just as his father used to try tricking me, when he was a toddler.

Unfortunately, that weekend before Christmas was the last time that I saw my grandson alive. Approximately six months later, he and his cousin were struck by a speeding driver. His cousin survived and we had that much for which we could thank God. But as for my grandson, the pain of losing him was crushing. We went through the motions of handling the best that we knew how. Death was no stranger to me, but there is something uniquely unexplainable about losing a child.

My son drove from North Carolina, where he was stationed in the military, to hook up with me for the trip back to the place that he called home. Together, we drove from Washington, DC to New Jersey. I knew that God had angels with us on that trip. First of all, I never go anywhere without asking Him to dispatch angels to be with me. I did most of the driving, until we made a stop for gas. It was not until then, that my son revealed that something was wrong with the car. At this point, my memory does not seem to serve me very accurately, but it seems that something was wrong with either the gas tank or the gas line. We had to wait several hours until it could be repaired before we could continue the trip. It was very late when we arrived at the home of his in-laws.

With God's help, we got through the week end as well as could be expected. My mother came up two days later on the train. It appeared that I was there, not only grieving for my grandson, but for ministry as well. Once it became known that I was an evangelist, I was put in the place of having to console and minister to other members of the family. There were a few people who "cornered me off", not only for consolation, but also for spiritual guidance. At least two of those recommitted their lives to Christ. My mother and I made a good team in that effort. We returned home on the train almost immediately after the funeral.

Although I was physically drained, it was good to be back home. Unfortunately, I was also emotionally drained. I was in the grieving process, which, for me, had to be delayed until after the funeral. I did well until the procession was taken by the family home. I was not aware that this was going to happen. When the procession stopped in front of the house, I said, "He will never play in that yard again or run through those doors again." I broke. I did not want the family to see me cry, but I could not stop the tears. I thought that I had to be strong enough to console all the others. Little did I realize that the family needed to see that I, too, was human and grieving even as they were. Coming home allowed me to begin ministering to myself. It was not easy at first. Some of my friends did not understand my loss. Therefore they did not know what to say to me. One put it this way – "It shouldn't be that hard for you. After all, you only knew him six months." At that moment, I became so angered by the remark that I wanted to hit her. I just walked away. Later, I explained to her how it could be so difficult. He was my grandson, no matter how long I had known him! It was difficult and I knew that I had to go through this process called grieving. **But God...**did not allow me to go through it alone. He was always there, sending me songs to sing and taking me to words of comfort, directly from His Word. He was, indeed, taking me higher. Some people say, "The higher the heights, the greater the fall." **But God....** He will never let me fall. Therefore, I will keep pressing on the upward way as He keeps taking me higher.

And it shall come to pass afterward, that I will pour out My Spirit on all flesh: Your sons and your daughters shall prophecy, your old men shall dream dreams, your young men shall see visions.

~ Joel 2:28, NKJV ~

CHAPTER TWENTY ONE:
Dreams, Visions, and Intuitions

The death of my grandson puts me in remembrance of what appears to be "giftings" in my family. I use the word "appears" because I think that my mother, oldest sister and I are/were "seers." I'm not sure about my mother, but as for me and my sister, these "gifts" were not readily recognized or fully understood by us. We didn't talk about them until much later in life. At the beginning of this book, I said that I could visualize images in the clouds. They were images of things that I heard about in Bible stories. I could see lambs, lions, chariots, etc. in the clouds. It was not until I was introduced to books with pictures, that I recognized what I had seen in the clouds.

I will start with the death of my grandson. Approximately one week before the accident, my mother was conducting a revival at my church. On the last night of the revival, as she was completing the benedictory prayer, she began to speak in tongues. She then told us that she saw a vision of an open casket (the full couch casket). She said that she also saw a "flash of blue" quickly passing the casket and that whoever was in the casket would be a very close family member of one of us who were present in the service that night.

When my grandson was killed, I never thought about the vision until my mother began asking questions about the details of his death. She asked about the color of the car and how fast it was moving. The car was blue and the driver had been speeding – "a flash of blue." My mother was convinced that this was the interpretation of her vision. My grandson was buried in a full couch casket. The funeral arrangements had been made before my mother arrived in New Jersey. She did not know that he was in an open casket until we went to the wake.

During our New Year Revival in 1982, again on the last night at the closing of the service, my mother had a vision of an explosion ("like something blew up over water"). The following Wednesday, a Boeing 737 crashed into the 14th Street Bridge between Washington, DC and Arlington, VA. These events were just a couple of the things that my mother would tell us about, before they happened.

As for me, there was little that I would talk about before it actually happened. The reason being was that when I began to see things, I thought that it was spooky and I didn't want people to think that I was crazy. When I first became aware of my enlightened moments, they were not dreams or visions. Instead, there were days filled with fear that "something bad was about to happen." I would become depressed by just wondering what it would be. Usually it would be the death of someone that I knew or someone getting hurt in an accident or fight. After the event (whatever happened), I would be fine.

I really didn't begin to pay a lot of attention to these unusual events until the early 1960's. I would push them aside as mere coincidences. However, I took special notice when President Kennedy was assassinated. I had been feeling really weird for a couple of days. On the day of his assassination, I was in such a state of anxiety that I kept telling my co-workers and my employer that something bad was about to happen. I couldn't seem to function because of the pressing thoughts that formed, but did not indicate what was about to happen. I went to lunch, but I did not eat. Instead, I went next door to the barbershop that was owned by a friend. I went to the back room and took a nap. When I went back to work my boss asked me if I still felt like something bad was going to happen. I told him "no." I hadn't noticed that the feeling was gone until he asked the question. I added that maybe I was just tired and had taken a nap during my lunch break. He tells me, "The next time you feel like something bad is going to happen, please don't come to work." The President had just been shot. I was stunned. My boss said something about being afraid of me. I don't know whether he was serious or not.

As I've previously stated, most of my intuitions involved death. Over the years, this became increasingly true. But the intuitions began to decrease and I began to dream as well as to have a few visions. The timing of my dreams or visions were too close to the actual events to be mere coincidences. Still, I didn't talk about most of the dreams because my family and friends thought that I was strange. I agreed. What was strange was that if I dreamed of someone that I knew who had died and that person talked to me in the dream, it was just a matter of a few weeks, sometimes days, before someone very close to me would die. If the person in the dream didn't talk to me, it was okay. For years, I lived in a dreadful state of anxiety because of my dreams that came to prepare me for someone's death.

Sometimes, I would not have a dream, but a sense of urgency concerning a particular person. For instance, my mother's sister was in the hospital and had been very ill. My last visit with her left me feeling that she was getting better. She told me that the doctors had said that she would be able to go home in less than a week. However, two days later, as I was cleaning my room, it was as though I could hear someone say "Go now if you want to see her again." I tried to ignore the thought, but it kept pressing, "Go now!" I stopped what I was doing and went to the hospital. It only took me twenty minutes to get there. I walked into the room in time to see them pull the covers over her head.

There were many other deaths in my family and among my friends that would have what I began to called "the warning." I will share a few of them. The day that my mother died, I knew that morning, when I got out of bed, that she would be dead before the next morning. I had had a continuous dream all night (another one of the "symptoms" of an impending negative event). If I awaken from a dream, during the night, the dream would continue when I went back to sleep. It would take too much to write the dream that I had the night before my mother died. I will just tell you what happened when I got up that next morning. It was Easter Sunday. It was also my brother's birthday and he had asked me to come to my mother's house early so that his family could take him to breakfast. My sisters, brother, and I took turns taking care of mother when we bought her home from the hospital. He would come on Saturday nights and stay until I got out of church on Sunday. Every Easter, my brother and his family would come back to my mother's house later in the afternoon. I agreed to come early as he had asked.

By this time, I had moved my membership to the church where I am currently a member. We were scheduled for an early morning service and the ministers were to serve breakfast afterward. During breakfast, I spoke with my co-pastor to tell her of my plans and asked to be excused from the regular service. What I really wanted to tell her was that my mother would not live for another twenty-four hours. My co-pastor had helped me to accept whatever God would allow concerning my mother's illness. I didn't want her to think that I was cracking under the pressure. So, I didn't mention the dream and what I knew that it meant.

When I arrive at my mother's house, my brother and I talked for a long while. He was late leaving for breakfast. I didn't tell what I knew to him either. I only shared with him what I received from my co-pastor, explaining how she had helped me. The day went smoothly. Mom had a few visitors. One of my sisters came to spend the night with me as she normally did on Sundays. After all of the visitors left, I told my sister to prepare for a rough night. She looked at me knowingly and asked, "You mean?" I said, "Yes." We both knew.

Mom's death came much quicker than I had expected. Somehow, I thought that it would be during the night. As it happened, it was partly as I dreamed. I was getting ready to clean her up for the night. As I was getting ready to change her, I notice that she had a vacant stare on her face. She did not respond to me calling her. I pulled back the curtain and told my sister that I thought she was dying. I called my mom once more. The response that I got was a long whispering sound as she breathed her last breath. I held my face to her nose. There was no breathing. It was over. No more pain and suffering for her. I couldn't say the same for me.

I knew that I had to be strong. Somehow, people get the idea that when you're a preacher or pastor, you're not supposed to hurt. I did my best not to show the pain. I made the necessary calls. I greeted my brother at the door. I had to let him know before he entered the house. Because I would not leave "my post", my mother's doctor kept checking to see if I was okay. I assured him that I was. I was as well as could be expected until they carried her out in a black leather bag.

Every time I think about the death of my mother, I thank God that we were able to engage in a loving relationship. I honestly believe that, had this not happened, I would have never been able to release the hatred that I had once held for her. Let me leave a warning here: Hatred is a horrid disease that will kill the very essence of your well-being. I have experienced it first-hand. I have seen it countless times in the counseling room, as I have ministered to people who refused to forgive someone for something that happened years, sometimes decades in the past.

If you are one of those persons who holds grudges and allows hatred to consume you, I urge you to let it go. If you hold to it, it will destroy you! Hatred can cause ill effects in your mind and will turn into bitterness. You will find yourself suffering from physical illnesses that are often the result of the mental stress that you allow, due to the lack of forgiveness. If you become angry every time you recall certain events or arguments, you are allowing that thing or that person too much control over your life. Forgiving someone is more for your benefit than it is for the one that you forgive. Even if a person doesn't want to accept your attempt to make things right, you can be released from the hurt and the pain. Allow God to cleanse/purify your thoughts and live life to the fullest. I didn't intend to preach here, but I know in my spirit that someone reading this book needs to release some things and in so doing, will be freed from the demons of your past.

Another dream that I want to tell you about had to do with my sister, although I didn't know it at the time that I'd had the dream. This too, was a continuing dream that occurred on a Sunday night. In the dream, I was laying in the street and looking up at something happening on the 11th Street Bridge in South East Washington, DC. There were police cars and ambulances but I could not tell exactly what was happening. I could only see the top of a car that was next to the wall of the bridge. I kept dreaming this dream throughout the night. The next day, I started making telephone calls to people that I knew who had a beige car. Two of them were my mother and my brother. They assured me that they were doing well and had not had an accident. On Tuesday, I was telling my sister about the dream. When I finished telling her about it, she asked me to confirm where I saw the event in my dream. She then told me that it was her. She was coming home from church that Sunday night. As she was crossing the bridge, her car started wobbling out of control about half way across (which would have been exactly the place that I saw). She said that her wheel came off of her car and that she lost control of it. She hit the side of the wall, which was the only thing that stopped the car. She relayed how frightened she had become. I never called her to tell her about the dream because I was focusing on a beige car. I did not make the connection that my sister's car was blue with a beige top.

As the years went by, my dreams and visions became clearer but fewer in number. Nonetheless, I would almost always know, in advance, when I had to prepare for the death of a loved one. I will admit that some did absolutely take me by surprise. I began to ask God not to let me struggle with the unknown. Now, I don't always get the warnings about the dying.

The last significant event that I will tell you about was not a dream. It was intuition. My son began having seizures about a year before he died. He would often fall down when they occurred. He had a seizure one day and the fall caused him to need medical attention. He was rushed to the hospital, where he experienced another seizure while talking to the doctor in the emergency room and went into a coma. For several days, he remained in the coma. My husband worked at the hospital and I would wait for him to get off work and we would leave together. On the night that he died, I sensed that he would not make it through the night. He didn't seem to be any worse. As a matter of fact, he was breathing more on his own. I could not get myself together. As I sat waiting for the next visit, I became anxious. There it was again, something bad was about to happen. It was 10:30pm when I left his room. My husband would be off in one-half hour, but I couldn't make myself wait. I was pressed to go home and I did. When my husband came home about an hour later, the phone rang as he walked in the door. The nurse told him that our son was taking a turn for the worse. It only took us fifteen minutes to get back to the hospital. When we walked in, I heard the ventilator flat line. He was gone. I've said it before and I say it again, there is something uniquely different about losing a child.

I wasn't the strong one this time. I had unanswered questions that caused me unusual grief. It took me a very long time to wrap my head around the fact that, just as my son was beginning to make a change in his life, his life was lost. He had even started going to church again. He would tell me that he was trying to get his life together. I'm ashamed to say that I became very angry. One morning, during my prayer time, I found myself yelling at God. "How can You let this happen to me? I'm the one who teaches people how to grieve! And here, I sit - a basket case, forcing myself to try to act normal." I fluctuated for about two years before I felt that I had experienced healing. But much to my surprise, I found out that I wasn't. It was Mother's Day, three years after my son's death. Co-Pastor was preaching. As I sat there listening, she made a statement that made me angry. It pertained to God saving our household. That was the one thing that bothered me. Had my son gotten saved before he died? I wanted to leave but couldn't. The next morning, again in my prayer time, I asked God if my son had gotten saved. The response was not what I wanted to hear: "That is between him and Me." Then I began to remember the final days that I had with him in the hospital and I do believe that he was able to make peace with God before he died. More importantly, I had to accept that whatever his state, it remained between him and God.

I continue to have intuitions, many of which have helped me tremendously in the counseling sessions. I'm also being helped by the dreams and visions. Times of crises can often make us question why God allows things to happen that cause us pain. But, I'm often reminded that I could never have come to this point in my life if it had not been for the many visions and dreams that I've had. They drew me closer to God and caused my prayer life to change in a marvelous way. Instead of praying with a defeatist attitude, I learned to pray with thanksgiving, realizing that God has been and always will be my deliverer. I could have lost it. I've stumbled along the way, **But God...** is my refuge and my strength, a very present help, whenever and wherever I need Him.

Years I spent in vanity and pride, Caring not my Lord was crucified, Knowing not it was for me He died On Calvary.

Mercy there was great, and grace was free; Pardon there was multiplied to me; There my burdened soul found liberty At Calvary.

By God's Word at last my sin I learned; Then I trembled at the law I'd spurned, Till my guilty soul imploring turned To Calvary.

Now I've giv'n to Jesus everything, Now I gladly own Him as my King, Now my raptured soul can only sing Of Calvary!

~ William R. Newell ~

CHAPTER TWENTY-TWO
Thanks To Calvary

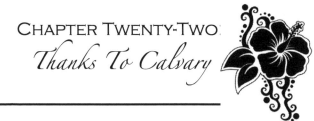

I've come a long way since joining that Pentecostal church when I was a teenager. I often say, "I was in the church, but the Church was not in me." For many years, I grew up in age and statue, but not in wisdom. Even when I gave my life to Christ (for real, for real), I knew that I had a lot of growing up to do. I stayed in the church where the Lord saved me for many years. I learned the value of Calvary. Christ set me free from victimization. The chains were broken, but I didn't know how to step out of them. Yes, I'd come a long way, but still had a long way to go.

I learned much from my lady pastor. She was the definition of "with loving kindness." I met many wonderful people in that little store-front church. I learned to look at many of them in different ways than I had previously. I came to realize that with the same manner that I judged others, I would also be judged. I also had to learn how to shut my mouth when I wanted to "give somebody a piece of my mind." I had to learn how to trust God, no matter what. I learn how to receive a sermon – not by how loud and how well the preacher could speak, or by how well the emotions of the people could be stirred up, but by the truth of the word that came forth.

I must admit that it was quite a challenge for me. I loved good music and I loved to dance. I was quite emotional. I danced so much that people thought that I was sick if I didn't dance. I had to pray about that. I asked the Lord to take some of my religion out of my feet and put more in my heart. The answer to that prayer was quite an experience. I began to notice that the relationship between me and my Savior was taking me to heights unknown. I praised Him, not only with a dance, but my walk and speech became different. I really began to better understand and appreciate the love that drove my Lord to Calvary.

I cannot express how much His love for me caused a definite change in me. From salvation to study of His Word, to preaching and teaching, I understood that it was not because of my being in the church. It was and is because of the sacrifice at Calvary that drew me to the place where He could put the Church in my heart. Thank God for Calvary!

In the early 1970's, I was introduce to another Calvary. I began to visit and fellowship with a church named Greater Mount Calvary Holy Church (GMCHC). After many years and much prayer, I moved my membership to that Church. One of my best friends who was with me the first time that I visited GMCHC, had become a member a few months after that first visit. I had the pleasure of getting to know Pastor and Co-pastor Owens on a personal level. They taught me so many things through that friendship as they shared unselfishly with me and my family. I had asked the Lord to break and reshape me into the image that I was created to be. This man and woman of God accepted me as I was and God used them as His instruments to point me to my purpose.

I remember saying to Bishop and Co-pastor Owens, "I have nothing to offer Calvary." He said to me, "It's not what you have to offer, it's what we can offer you." Indeed! It would take several additional chapters to tell about all of the marvelous benefits that they have afforded me. I will forever be grateful to them for all the opportunities that they have given me and for the doors that have been opened to me because of their leadership. Yes, thanks to my Lord who died on Calvary AND thanks to my leaders at GMCHC, Archbishop Alfred A. Owens, Jr. and Co-Pastor Susie C. Owens.

There are many other wonderful members of my family at GMCHC who have also be instrumental in my growth in ministry. They are too many to mention by name, but I would be remiss not to mention Bishop T. Cedric Brown and Elder Bobette Brown. They, too, are a great source of inspiration as I watch them in ministry together. I appreciate their influence in my life. I'll use the phrase that Bishop Brown so often uses: "good leaders are a blessing; bad leaders are a curse." I'm certainly blessed to sit under such good leaders.

To all of my family at GMCHC, thank each of you so much for your love, prayers, respect, and support. God has blessed me in so many ways – giving me spiritual children who help me with the assignments that God has given me, sisters and brothers to encourage me, and so much more. Thank you Calvary!

I'm free, Praise the Lord I'm free. I'm no longer bound, no more chains holding me. My soul is resting and it's just a blessing. Praise the Lord, Hallelujah, I'm free.

~ Rev. Milton Bronson and Thompson Community Choir ~

CHAPTER TWENTY THREE:
No More Dysfunction

At the beginning of this book, I promised to tell you more about God's family. **God will have His family as He intended from the beginning.** It will be a family that will not be dysfunctional – a family that will live in peace and harmony. Family members will love one another even as He loves us. He will be pleased to call us His children. With the world in which we live becoming more and more dysfunctional on a daily basis, some may wonder just how God is going to have this perfect family. Let me start by saying this – Our God is an awesome, sovereign God. He is not a loser. If He declares a thing, it will certainly come to pass. As dysfunctional as some of us are, God has made it possible for us to change. Christ did not come as a failure. His dying was not in vain. Our fore-parents may have failed, but there is no failure in God. Christ came to do for us what we could not do for ourselves – free us from our dysfunctional ways.

Soon, there is going to be the greatest family gathering that has ever been. The gathering will be so large that we will have to spend an eternity getting around to all of our family members and that's just the way God intends for it to be. He wants us to spend eternity with Him. However, the choice is ours, whether or not we will inherit the promise of eternal life. Unfortunately, some of us will be banned from the family unit because we refuse to release our dysfunctional attitudes. Again, the choice remains with us. God has made it possible, through the shed blood of Jesus Christ, for any to be free from all of our dysfunctions. No matter what we've done, we can receive the inheritance that our Father has laid up for us.

I have a special word for those of you who have been abused and violated sexually. God was not the one who harmed you! It was the works of the devil. Let me tell you what I've learned through all that I've written in this book: What the devil meant for evil, God can turn it around and use it for your good. He did it for me and, if you will allow Him, He will do it for you. If you intend to be a part of God's perfect family, you will have to release hatred, bitterness, and low self-esteem. You are a survivor! Don't just exist – live! Live your life to the fullness in Christ. Say as the psalmist said, "I shall not die, but live and declare the works of the Lord" (Psalm 118:17).

Do you really want to be healed or have you lost all hope? Are you afraid to trust God because it appears that your waiting for a breakthrough is in vain? How long has it been? Ten, twenty, thirty or more years? Have you stopped praying about your infirmity and accepted it as something that you will just have to live with? The devil is a liar! You don't have to remain stuck in that pit. How long will you continue to suffer the anguish? Have you honestly given it to God? Oh! Maybe you're angry with Him because you can't seem to hear from Him as it relates to your pain? At this point, none of that should matter. God is able to do exceedingly, abundantly, above all that we ask or think.

I'll ask you again – do you really want to be healed, set free, and delivered or do you continue hold to your infirmity even as God is telling you to release it? Would you continue to clutch a knife with which you have just cut yourself or would you let it go and attend to the wound? It is necessary for you to drop it – let it go! Sometimes, a wound is so serious that it requires a visit to your physician. If the physician is proficient, he or she will attend to the wound, thoroughly cleansing it, and applying whatever remedy is necessary to begin the healing process. If needed, the wound would be stitched in order to facilitate a more rapid closure of the flesh so that the scar from the wound would be less noticeable. No intelligent, caring physician would leave a gaping wound to heal on its own. A good physician would take care to cover the wound to protect it from becoming infected. If infection occurs, the outcome could be more dangerous than the initial cause of the wound.

When the doctor has finished all that needs to be done, the patient is given instructions for proper home care – how to change the bandage (covering) and how to apply additional ointment. Prescriptions may be given to help alleviate the pain. The patient may be required to go back to the doctor for professional evaluations of the healing process.

The reason that some of you have not been healed is because you refuse to go to the doctor to receive the proper care for the wound. The wound has become infected and you are getting sicker instead of better. Why not allow our Lord, the Chief Physician, to treat that gaping hole in your heart. You've been hurt and scarred. You're not experiencing the healing process because you are not getting the proper care. The wounded area needs a spiritual cleansing, a healing ointment has to be applied, and the wound must be covered for protection. Medication may be needed to alleviate the pain. I am a witness that Dr. Jesus can do all that needs to be done to heal your broken spirit. He can work miracles in your life. He can cleanse you by His Word and cover you with His feathers. He will take you under His wings and protect you (see Psalm 91).

When there is a serious wound, the patient will have to go back to the physician for follow up treatments during the healing process. You will need to do the same. If you do not follow through with your treatments, the healing will be incomplete. Keep going back to Jesus in prayer, thanking Him as He gently removes the scar tissue. Keep going back for follow up until your heart no longer hurts. Keep going back until you can experience the joy that only Christ can give.

As you are receiving treatment for your wounds, you may be scarred for a period of time. The time does not have to be prolonged if you allow yourself to forgive the person(s) who wounded you. The sooner you forgive, the sooner the scars will heal and clear up. Forgiveness is absolutely necessary to obtain complete healing. You cannot afford to hold on to hatred. It will hurt you more. You should not expect to get revenge on the person(s) who left you bleeding. God said that vengeance belongs to Him. He said that He will repay. He will give you back everything that the devil stole from you or even something better. He will make you brand new and completely whole. He can, if you allow Him, give you joy unspeakable. There is no pain that He cannot heal. I tell you what I know. Release the past. It may not be easy, but with God, it can be done. There is no failure in Him.

The need for forgiveness of others may cause you some mental anguish. If you need assistance, find a Christian counselor or therapist who can walk along beside you as you allow the Holy Spirit to free your mind from the negative circumstances that caused your pain. Talking confidentially with someone who will help you pray through is half of the battle that will bring you to victory through Christ Jesus. My prayer for you is that even as He has done for me, He will do for you. I want to leave this prayer for you as you step into your place of victory in Christ Jesus:

The Lord bless you and keep you; the Lord make His face shine upon you, and be gracious to you; The Lord lift up His countenance upon you, and give you peace (Numbers 6:24-26).

No more dysfunction! That's my testimony –The chains are broken and I have stepped out of them!

My Testimony

I would like to start my testimony with the following illustration: A homeless person, who has no friend, has wallowed in the filthy streets until she became dirty, smelly and much in need of a bath and fresh clothing. Someone comes along and takes her (just as she is) to a beautiful home, draws up a bubble bath for her and gives her nice clean clothes to put on. Then she is set down at a table that has an abundance of food which has been prepared just for her. The homeless person has her needs met and expresses her gratitude by continuously thanking her hostess and inquiring if there is anything that she can do to show her appreciation. The hostess merely replies, "Just share what you have received with others by bringing them to my house." (Author unknown)

I feel that I can relate to this illustration. I had a physical building in which to live but spiritually, I was homeless. I had decided to leave the church and forsake the principles of God. I was soiled and miserable because I wandered off into some dark place. Someone came to rescue me. It was the Spirit of God. He led me to a place of refreshment, washed the dirt away, and began to feed me. I wanted to show my appreciation for this great kindness that was shown to me and decided that I would be the Lord's servant for the rest of my life.

Since making that decision, God has blessed me beyond my greatest imaginations. My experience, as His servant, has been rewarding in every aspect of my life. I have been in the preaching and teaching ministry for 33 years. I served as an assistant and co-pastor in the church where I grew up. I went back to school and obtained (as my final degree) a Doctorate in Ministry.

Currently, I am serving at the Greater Mt. Calvary Holy Church in Washington, DC, under the greatest pastors in the world – Archbishop Alfred A. Owens, Jr. and Co-Pastor Susie C. Owens, in the following positions: Pastoral lay counselor; Elder on the board of the Ministerial Alliance (emeritus); President of the missionary ministry; Instructor in our Bible School (Calvary Bible Institute). In addition, I have been blessed with a position as an adjunct professor at National Bible College and Seminary in Fort Washington, MD.

I've come to this point in my life, not through any goodness of my own, but through the compassionate mercy of God. When I look back over my life, I can only say that it is because of the Lord's mercies that I was not consumed (overtaken by the tricks of the adversary). God has been good to me (in spite of myself) and has kept me up to this point. He has allowed me to share the blessing of salvation and redemption with others as I invite them into His house.

I cannot thank Him enough for how He has blessed me. Only God could have made the necessary changes in my life that have caused me to set as **my number one priority the desire to please Him**. I have chosen to surrender my life and my will to the will of God as I endeavor to serve Him and minister to others. I've come to realize that it's not about me, but about the purpose that God has for me. **MY MOTTO FOR LIFE IS: "IN HIS SERVICE FOR HIS GLORY."**

Satan thought that he had me...**BUT GOD! HE BROKE THE CHAINS OF MY BROKEN SPIRIT AND RESCUED ME FROM THE HANDS OF THE ENEMY! PRAISE JESUS!!!!!!!!!!!!!**

ABOUT THE AUTHOR

IN HIS SERVICE FOR HIS GLORY

ELDER JACKIE RICE, a native of Washington, DC, is a member of the Greater Mt. Calvary Holy Church (GMCHC), under the leadership of Archbishop Alfred A. Owens, Jr. and Co-Pastor Susie C. Owens. She has been in the teaching/preaching ministry for thirty-three years. She serves as a member of the Ministerial Alliance (emeritus) of GMCHC, and as President of the GMCHC Missionary Board.

As a member of the American Association of Christian Counselors, Elder Rice is a Certified Lay Counselor, ministering primary to adult and young adult women. She also serves as a volunteer counselor for CSOSA (Court Services and Offender Supervision Agency) in Washington, DC, ministering to inmates who are returning to the community. She has previously served in the capacity of Sunday School teacher, as the Overseer of GMCHC Youth Ministry, as a Senior Counselor with Calvary's Big Sister Mentoring Program (working with young ladies between the ages of twelve and twenty), and as a team leader on the Ministerial Alliance at GMCHC.

Prior to GMCHC, Elder Rice served as the Assistant Pastor at the Silver Temple Pentecostal Holiness Church in Washington, DC. She has taught Bible Study classes at various churches in the Washington, DC area. Her ministry has included travel throughout the United States as well as to Trinidad, West Indies.

Elder Rice is a product of the District of Columbia public schools. She has obtained an Associate Degree in Religious Education from the Washington Saturday College, a Master of Divinity, and a Doctorate of Ministry from Faith Christian University & Schools in the State of Maryland. In addition to her studies, Elder Rice was also an instructor at Faith Christian University & Schools.

Currently, Elder Rice is employed at GMCHC, as a pastoral lay counselor. She teaches at Calvary Bible Institute and is an adjunct professor at National Bible College and Seminary in Fort Washington, MD. She is retired from PSI International Corporation as a Quality Analyst on FDA contracts (Drug Safety and Surveillance).

Elder Rice is the proud mother of four children, six grandchildren, and four great-grandchildren. God has also blessed her with many spiritual children and grandchildren who affectionately call her "Mother" or "Mom" Rice. She loves the Lord and her greatest joy is pursuing her "PHD" – that is to PLEASE HIM DAILY.

CONTACT INFORMATION:

Dr. Rice wants to hear from you! E-mail your
questions or comments at gusnme1971@comcast.net

Proverbs 3:5-6
"Trust in the Lord
with all your heart
and lean not on
your own under-
standing; in all your
ways submit to him,
and he will make
your path straight."